Bobbi*,
 I hope this book meets
you where you are and
encourages you! May the
love of Jesus surround you
on your journey set apart
yet full of purpose!
He called you by name!

♡ Matt Book

Raising Special Stars

SIXTEEN WEEKS OF EMPOWERMENT FOR MOMS RAISING CHILDREN WITH SPECIAL NEEDS

Mattie Book

WESTBOW
PRESS®
A DIVISION OF THOMAS NELSON
& ZONDERVAN

WestBow Press books may be ordered through booksellers or by contacting:

WestBow Press
A Division of Thomas Nelson & Zondervan
1663 Liberty Drive
Bloomington, IN 47403
www.westbowpress.com
844-714-3454

Scripture quotations taken from The Holy Bible, New International Version® NIV®
Copyright © 1973 1978 1984 2011 by Biblica, Inc. TM. Used
by permission. All rights reserved worldwide.
by permission. All rights reserved.

Scripture quotations marked (NLT) are taken from the Holy Bible,
New Living Translation, copyright © 1996, 2004, 2007 by Tyndale
House Foundation. Used by permission of Tyndale House Publishers,
Inc., Carol Stream, Illinois 60188. All rights reserved.

ISBN: 978-1-6642-0611-3 (sc)
ISBN: 978-1-6642-0612-0 (hc)
ISBN: 978-1-6642-0610-6 (e)

Library of Congress Control Number: 2020918200

Print information available on the last page.

WestBow Press rev. date: 10/12/2020

For my daughters, Hannah and Elaina

You two shine bright like the stars and have inspired me more than you will ever know. I am forever grateful to be your mom.

Contents

Foreword

Have you ever desired to be somewhere other than where you currently are? A new destination? A new perspective? A new heart posture? Do you yearn for clear steps to carry you there?

Mattie Book invites us into those steps—strides of hopeful possibility, joy, and true transformation. She invites us in because she herself takes those steps toward our heavenly Father, whom she has grown to trust immensely and steps toward carrying His love to people. Mattie radiates Jesus's love as she tenderly holds her sweet children's hands, listens—like really listens to people's stories—and beckons us all to see moments of delight and joy in the unseen treasures of each day. May you relish the encounter of her contagious positivity and vision of loving truth for each family as you dive into the journey of the following pages.

Both you and your child have a remarkable place in God's redemptive story. Mattie believes you can see God's intentionality, feel His presence, and trust His love. I do too.

You are seen and entrusted to care for each precious child lovingly placed in your family.

As you desire goodness amid darkness, power amid helplessness, and nearness amid isolation, may you experience Mattie's heart for stories of God's invitation, belonging, and *fullness* for *each* of us.

What God begins, He will complete. Let's look up together.

Ang Bryant

Acknowledgments

First, I want to thank Jesus for giving me the stars to gaze at on the darkest of nights. Thank You for using our hardships for good and for giving me identity, belonging, and purpose in Your kingdom. Thank You for equipping me time and time again and for teaching me to walk above the chaos. Thank You for seeing me when I felt the rest of the world didn't, and thank You for using my gifts to pursue the few. I am a wife, mom, nurse, and friend, but I will always be your daughter first!

A special thank-you to my husband, Zachary, for all the love and support you give to your family. You lead our family to the feet of Jesus every day, and I cherish you. I could never thank you enough for all you do to be an intentional husband and father. I fall more in love with you every day.

Also, a special thank-you to my best friend, Tabitha, for being willing to visit Holland so frequently. You love our family in action and in truth. I will always be thankful for our friendship. Thank you for seeing the wine in my glass when all I could see was the water!

Introduction

I once read an essay, "Welcome to Holland," that I could relate to. It described the journey of having a child with special needs. Once I read it, I felt like a piece of my heart was home, like everything I had always tried to explain to everyone about our journey was described perfectly. God knew as I read it that in time I wouldn't just think about it. I'd actually write a book to all the women who lived in this place called Holland. I had to journey a little bit, though, and figure my way around. I had to look up and see the stars when it got dark. I had to meet with Jesus in places I never imagined I would go. This essay is special to me, and I believe it will be special to you too.

***

Welcome to Holland
©1987 by Emily Perl Kingsley. All rights reserved. Reprinted by permission of the author.

I am often asked to describe the experience of raising a child with a disability—to try to help people who have not shared that unique experience to understand it, to imagine how it would feel. It's like this ... ...

When you're going to have a baby, it's like planning a fabulous vacation trip—to Italy. You buy a bunch of guide books and make your wonderful plans. The Coliseum. The Michelangelo David. The gondolas in Venice. You may learn some handy phrases in Italian. It's all very exciting.

After months of eager anticipation, the day finally arrives. You pack your bags and off you go. Several hours later, the plane lands. The flight attendant comes in and says, "Welcome to Holland."

"Holland?!?" you say. "What do you mean Holland?? I signed up for Italy! I'm supposed to be in Italy. All my life I've dreamed of going to Italy."

But there's been a change in the flight plan. They've landed in Holland and there you must stay.

The important thing is that they haven't taken you to a horrible, disgusting, filthy place, full of pestilence, famine and disease. It's just a different place.

So you must go out and buy new guide books. And you must learn a whole new language. And you will meet a whole new group of people you would never have met.

It's just a different place. It's slower-paced than Italy, less flashy than Italy. But after you've been there for a while and you catch your breath, you look around ... and you begin to notice that Holland has windmills ... and Holland has tulips. Holland even has Rembrandts.

But everyone you know is busy coming and going from Italy ... and they're all bragging about what a wonderful time they had there. And for the rest of your life, you will say "Yes, that's where I was supposed to go. That's what I had planned."

And the pain of that will never, ever, ever, ever go away ... because the loss of that dream is a very very significant loss.

But ... if you spend your life mourning the fact that you didn't get to Italy, you may never be free to enjoy the very special, the very lovely things ... about Holland.

***

I have found that living in my Holland, a land I never would have chosen, has given me the opportunity to develop an unwavering faith, an anchored hope, and an inspiring perseverance. In Holland, I was given different views to savor and various perspectives to consider. I may have never chosen to raise our family in this place called Holland, but I have decided to see the rainbows and cling to God's promises in the land I never knew I would reside. The Bible has become my map for navigating through the many unknowns in our journey, and Jesus has taken my hand to lead me through the hills and valleys of a place I never expected to be.

But it wasn't always that way. Every morning my little girls run into our room when they wake up. They yell, "Mommy, Mommy, we're awake. Can we go watch TV now?" Sometimes I say yes, and other times I yell back for them to go back to bed—you know, those mornings when they bombard us at 5:00 a.m.

Sometimes I tell them to go find a book instead. Other times, when I know we have a long day ahead, I just tell them to come cuddle with me for a minute. Regardless of the answer, two things are always true: they always run into our room first, and they always ask me what's next.

One day as my girls came charging into our room before dawn, God spoke to me. "Mattie, what if you came running into my presence like your girls run to you? What if your first stop of the day was my throne? Now go write this down for the women in Holland."

I started running to His throne every day. For me, this meant opening my eyes in the morning, just to close them right away and enter into prayer. I started asking God to take me to His throne. I say that I began "running" to His throne because the process of entering into prayer was quick. I didn't waste time. My heart started chasing the heart of God.

After I asked God to take me to His throne, I would envision sitting at the bottom of a beautiful bright-white marble staircase that led up to God's throne. I imagined sitting in God's presence, a place of peace and power. I would pour out my heart to God in prayer, and then I would wait. I learned to be still and to listen.

Throughout the day, I would spend time in scripture. I began seeking Him with my whole heart in a pursuit to hear Him. A relational God created us. For so long, I had this subconscious belief that God stopped talking to His people in the book of Revelation. After the Bible was completed, nobody was worthy of hearing Him speak. Oh, was I wrong!

Our God who created the heavens and the earth created us and delights in us. He is a God that speaks! When I learned to listen for His voice, I began to hear it, and He started filling my heart with treasures of truth—riches to reflect on, write about, and share with you.

God sees you in your journey. He is proud of you, sister, and He wants to invite you into a sixteen-week journey of looking up and being lavished in His love. So this is your invitation. Your journey as a special needs mama is one that is set apart. Jesus wants you to delight in His rest and become empowered in the journey you find yourself in. He wants you to soar through the days ahead and be confident that He cherishes you and your child.

So let's spend the next sixteen weeks ahead running daily to God's throne and receiving all He has for us. Let's get empowered and use our story for His glory.

This sixteen-week Bible study starts with the first week, "Look Up, Love," the foundation for the remaining fifteen weeks. Then it is structured in four sections:

- Section 1 focuses on the scriptures of John 11 and the resurrecting hope many of us are desperate for as well as the reality of Jesus entering into the darkest of places.

- Section 2 is full of encouragement for persevering through the obstacles and hardships we can find ourselves in.

- Section 3 is a discussion of the healing stories of Jesus and the guidance we have with the Holy Spirit as we make the hard decisions and plan for an unknown future.

- Section 4 is a general reflection of our entire journey as special needs mothers. We dive into Matthew 14, a story of an unplanned storm. During our time in section 4, we will look at the many ways that God plans on using our stories to inspire others and empower us in our days ahead.

Each week ends with a prayer and five reflection questions. This book can be read independently as well as in small-group settings.

All too often special needs moms are isolated and in need of community. If you are reading this independently, I want you to know you aren't alone. God is with you as you read every word, and He led me to write this book as if we were sitting together at a coffee shop sharing truth and drinking iced coffees. If you are reading this in a small-group setting, I want to let you know that I am pumped for all the ways you and your group are going to grow together. Your stories are all different, and yet God brought you all together for a purpose.

As you enter into the next sixteen weeks, know that I am praying for each of you. I am confident that God will speak to each of you and through this Bible study you will learn to hear His voice and apply His Word as your manual for a journey that didn't come with one.

Love,

Mattie Book

Week 1

Look Up, Love

Look up into the heavens. Who created all the stars? He brings them out like an army, one after another, calling each by its name. Because of his great power and incomparable strength, not a single one is missing.

— ISAIAH 40:26 (NLT)

I wish I could tell you that it is always sunny and seventy-five in Holland, but that wouldn't be true. That isn't true for Italy either. I know sometimes we think Italy is a perfect place without rain, but it hails there as well. I have friends who live there and tell me it actually isn't always perfect. The weather is always changing, and right when one season ends, another begins. Holland is different from Italy, though. There are different mountains to climb, views to see, and winds to blow our way. If you are reading this and wondering why I am talking about Holland and Italy it's all explained in a beautiful essay in the introduction. Our plane landed in Holland about seven years ago. We have had quite the adventure.

Our daughters have Joubert syndrome, a rare condition. The first time I had ever heard of it was when they were diagnosed. It poses a high risk of kidney and liver disease and causes a lot of disabilities. The challenges and obstacles that my girls face are not things that I could have ever prepared for. I have grieved the loss of the life I thought I would have as well as the possibility of losing our girls to the vicious diseases that often make their way into kids with Joubert syndrome.

For so long I became accustomed to looking down. Both my children and I were always picked last. Nobody wanted to enter my world, but I was desperate to enter theirs. Although every time I tried, I was just reminded that I didn't belong. I was a special needs mom; I lived in the unknown. All that I had dreamed motherhood would be had changed.

God found me in Holland. He reminded me that although my journey of motherhood is always changing, He stays the same. When I have to survive the chaos, He provides the constant. When everyone in my life just can't understand, He does. When I show up with my two fish, He supplies the rest. When all I see are burdens, He shows me blessings. One thing I have found to be true is that God isn't afraid of Holland. He actually treasures it.

I started asking God to show me who I am. I needed Him to speak identity into me. I asked Him to take away anything I was believing about myself that wasn't true and fill my heart with what He had spoken over me from the start.

Gentle and gracious, God said the words "set apart." For the first time in my life, I knew a piece of my identity. I was set apart—not better or less than. I want to emphasize *not less than* because while being a mom with kids who have disabilities, I often do feel less than. But no, I'm not less than. I'm set apart. You are too.

I needed God to show me "set apart" in scripture. He is kind and present, so He did. He showed me the star that shone so bright shortly after Jesus was born, the star that the wise men followed. This star was different from the rest but full of purpose. Many people looked up into the dark sky that night and didn't appreciate the way it shined differently or moved among the rest. But the wise men looked up and saw it as set apart and set in the sky by God.

They chose that special set-apart star and followed it to Jesus.

Matthew 2:10 (NLT) reads, "When they saw the star, they were filled with joy!" Our stories and journeys are different. We all entered motherhood with dreams and expectations, and a lot of us have had to redream and let go of the expectations that once harbored in our hearts. Many of us have wrestled with God, and many of us have been wounded by others. Some of us still can't go back to church, and others lead Bible studies for moms every week. A few of us live in Holland full-time with all of our kids, and some of us live in Holland part-time with one child as we find balance with our other children who were born in Italy. But we have all walked the streets at one point or another with our heads down, feeling less than.

I want to invite you to see the stars again and to look up and be reminded for the next sixteen weeks that even in the darkest nights, God gave us the stars. I want you to experience God's promises in your journey that you never truly knew belonged to you and to find empowerment in your days ahead. I want your story to burn brightly as it is *set apart* from the rest. It just may be the star that leads a few to the King. So whether you are doing this by yourself or in a small group, I invite you to see the stars and be reminded that just as God calls the stars by name, He has called YOU by name as well. He has called you to raise your special stars to shine in the brilliant way they were created to shine and to lead a life full of purpose!

As I was writing this Bible study, God specifically told me to share one-third of my story and two-thirds of His story. God also put questions on my heart to ask at the end of each week as an opportunity for you to reflect on your own personal journey. Each of our stories matter to the heart of God and are filled with purpose. Let's run to God's throne every day together for the next sixteen weeks. Let's be held and let Him fill our hands, eyes, and hearts with His treasures. Let's give these next sixteen weeks our all and watch as God shows us again and again that He really is who He says He is—near, present, loving, and helpful.

God showed me a vision of women looking up and seeing the wonder, joy, and promises of God as they dived into each section. When you look up, your whole posture changes. Let's change the postures of our journeys. Let's live in a way that when the world would see a million reasons for us to look down, it views us looking up with our hands raised to the God who fills our eyes with sight, hands with treasures, and hearts with joy.

I encourage you to meditate on Isaiah 40:26 this week and ask God to show you all the treasure in this scripture. Ask Him to speak your identity into your heart and to show you how He views your journey as a special needs mom. Run to His throne every morning and let Him speak truth into your day.

Prayer

Heavenly Father, we love You and are going to trust You. I ask that every woman reading this book spends the next sixteen weeks running to Your throne and looking up. Fill their hands with treasures and their days with joy. I ask that You speak to them through this journey and reveal to them how their stories are set apart for Your glory. I ask that You uproot any false identities in their hearts and grow truth.

Show them that they are Your daughters and that You have created the stars for them to marvel at in the darkest of nights. Bring people into their lives to encourage them and speak life into them. I thank You for all the ways they will experience Your goodness and find strength in Your faithfulness for the days to come. God, thank You for loving Holland and all the women in it. In Jesus's name. Amen.

Reflection Questions

When you found out you were going to be a special needs mom, what thoughts consumed you?

What will our family look like now? Finances. Tristan... will he be ok with his brother needing more attention? The unknowns... Will he have a career? Will he find love? Will he be able to smile? Will he be OK? my mind was racing.

Have you found God in your journey yet? If yes, when and where?

Through my moms group at church. Particularly this past week. God chose me to be Lincoln's mom. I am to guide him to God and to unconditionally love him. I need to trust in him and his plan. I cannot do it all.

When you read Matthew 2:10, what comes to mind?

God sets examples, images, physical things in our life as a reminder of Him. I feel holding or seeing something as a physical reminder of his light, love, and power helps us grow closer to him.

Many people will walk past you every day and not notice the purpose in your set-apart journey, but others will see God's faithfulness shining through your story and actually be led to Him. When is a time that His faithfulness has been bright in a dark night?

_____

_____

_____

_____

_____

How do you see your special stars shine daily?

When Lincoln smiles at me, Or tries to crawl, his giggle and laugh. All these things I never knew if he'd be able to do or not. He has God's light in his eyes. He is pure, innocent, loving. I never knew how I could love my 2nd child as much as my first, but there's and unexplainable, special place in my heart God has given me for Lincoln.

Treasures of the Week (Notes)

We are headed into our first week. Ladies, I am excited for this journey. Run to God's throne this week. You are not only invited but also wanted! He is waiting for you to run to Him this week. Ask Him to prepare your heart this week and to speak identity into your heart. Your kids' journeys are set apart and full of purpose.

I believe that we are on this journey together. Invite God to speak to you this week, and then write it all down. Let's look up and see the stars.

God placed them in the sky for those who choose to see in the dark.

-Spread my love to others in need.

_____

_____

_____

_____

_____

_____

_____

_____

As You Go on Your Way

The stars are like a souvenir of God's promises. During the day when light covers the atmosphere from the sun, the stars aren't seen, but they are still very much hovering over us, ready to shine in their own unique way when darkness comes at night. The stars don't leave during the day and certainly don't leave in the night. In the same way, God's promises never leave us. His promise to love, sustain, redeem, choose, strengthen, and never forsake us surrounds us every day and night of our lives. When the skies are bright and we can see our way, we can rest in knowing God's promises surround us.

When the skies turn black and we don't know our way, we can be reminded that His promises are a guiding light, a treasure of His love that He placed in the sky for us even before we were born. He created the stars before He created humankind to make sure that none of His beloved children would ever live a life in the dark. His light is always present; sometimes it just takes some dark nights to see it clearly.

It wasn't until I was in the darkest nights of my life that I witnessed His promises shining the brightest. As you travel through each section of this book, please note that I placed a verse about the stars at the bottom of each section's introduction page. I want you to put this verse in your pocket and pull it out from time to time as you go through each section. Reflect on it and be reminded that sometimes you don't get the opportunity to see the stars clearly until the night sky goes dim. Occasionally you have to enter into the times of the unknown to clearly see the promises of a known God.

Section 1

In section 1, we will study John 11. For the next four weeks, we will be reflecting on the presence of Jesus in our pain and the many ways we cope with loss and uncertainty. The story of Lazarus rising from the dead shows us the power of Jesus entering into our dark places and resurrecting hope into our journeys. We will also look at Lazarus's sisters and the way they ventured through a time they never expected to be in.

#HISPRESENCEISAPRESENTINTHEPRESENT
#ASISTERONTHEMOVE
#THESISTERTHATSTAYED
#WORTHTHESTOP

The sun has one kind of splendor, the moon another and the stars another; and star differs from star in splendor.

— 1 CORINTHIANS 15:41 (NIV)

Week 2

Lazarus: His Presence is a Present in the Present

This week's scripture is John 11. Yes, love, we are reading the whole thing! There is so much for us in the story of Lazarus. Over the next four weeks, we are going to explore John 11 and gather all the treasures of truth that can be found in a story that is full of loss, love, sisterhood, and the presence of Jesus that is found in the darkest of times. This week we are going to lean into a verse that is simple yet full of power. It's known to be the shortest verse in scripture, "Jesus wept" (John 11:35 NIV).

Throughout my journey, I have cried out to God many times. I have begged for answers about the past. "God, why were they diagnosed? Why our children? Why did You allow this to happen to us?" And I have also cried out about the future. "Lord, please let my daughters experience friendship. Jesus, please give them a future. In Jesus's name, I pray that my girls would walk, talk, and praise your name." I so often pray about what is coming next. My prayer space is full of questions and requests to God. I have done this routine for years. Either I am wailing about the past or pleading for the future.

When I was reading through John 11, something beautiful happened when I read the words "Jesus wept" (John 11:35 NIV). Jesus stopped me as I read that line, and tears filled my eyes. The truth of this single sentence filled my heart. I had discovered that for twenty-eight years, I had missed one of the greatest gifts Jesus offers us, the present.

When Jesus was with His disciples two days before Lazarus' death, He told them in John 11:4 that Lazarus's life wouldn't end in death. Jesus knew as He entered the town and Martha came running up to Him that Lazarus would walk out of the tomb at the end of the day. He knew the future even in the past tense. Jesus knew that Lazarus, whom He loved, would not remain dead but instead be woken up and God would be glorified. So why then would Jesus weep? Why would Jesus, the Son of the living God, weep when He knew that Lazarus would rise from the dead and walk out of the tomb victoriously?

As I thought of this question, I prayed and asked

God to show me. He shared with my heart, "My presence is a present in the present." Jesus saw people He loved hurting. Even though He knew that a miracle was moments away, He wept anyway. Why? Because Jesus doesn't just want to be in our past and in our future. He wants to be in our present. He wants to meet you where you are and be in that space.

So many times through our special journey I have become bitter with people who always want to dismiss my present. I have been fearful of the loss of my girls, and they will say things like, "I know God has a plan for this" or "God won't give you anything more than you can handle." These aren't things that are deliberately said to hurt me, but they aren't helpful. Why? Because sometimes I just need someone to look me in the eye and tell me he or she sees our challenging situation and it breaks that person's heart too. I don't need to hear about the future working out or God thinking I'm superwoman. I need someone just to sit and cry with me.

Jesus wept. He showed us in that moment how present He is. Jesus knew His hands were about to raise this man from the dead and there was no reason to weep, yet He wept anyway. He did this to be present with His people. He still does this. There hasn't been a time yet in this journey that

He wasn't waiting to weep with me. It's a present, though, and not all of us unwrap it. We blame Him for the past or cry out for the future, and we miss the present.

It's okay to weep and to cry out about the unimaginable. Loss is hard. As special needs moms, we grieve so often the lives we thought we'd experience as moms. It's a true loss. When we weep, Jesus isn't just in the future or past. He's in that moment. He wants to give you the present of His presence in the present. He walked to the town, wept with the people, and woke up Lazarus. The present was never missed, and neither is yours. Invite him in. Let Him weep with you. He is the only one who can weep with you over the unimaginable and then do unimaginable. He loved you, He loves you, and He will continue loving you.

Prayer

Heavenly Father, Your love for us is abounding. You never miss a moment with Your people. I just ask that every heart would be opened to You. I ask that Your love would meet us in our weeping and laughter, that we would welcome You and feel Your presence in all our moments. Jesus, thank You for weeping with Your people and choosing the present in a moment when people were so focused on the past and the future. Please continue to meet us where we are at. We love You, Lord. Amen.

Reflection Questions

What are some specific things that others have told you that weren't helpful when you were hurting in your journey?

_____

_____

_____

_____

_____

What do you grieve in your journey?

_____

_____

_____

_____

_____

What do you think is the significance of Jesus weeping with His people?

_____

_____

_____

_____

_____

How can you be intentional in inviting Jesus into your moments this week?

_____

_____

_____

_____

_____

Look back on your journey. Name at least three times you have been stuck in grief. Next to it, write where Jesus was. If you don't know, then let's pray this week that Jesus will show you where He was in those moments.

_____

_____

_____

_____

_____

Treasures of the Week (Notes)

Yay! Week two is underway. Feel free to jot down what God is up to through the week. What is God speaking to you in your journey? What burdens have you been carrying to His table? What blessings are you receiving?

_____

_____

Lazarus: His Presence is a Present in the Present

_____

_____

_____

_____

_____

_____

_____

_____

Week 3

Martha: A Sister on the Move

When Martha heard that Jesus was coming, she went out to meet him, but Mary stayed at home. "Lord," Martha said to Jesus, "if you had been here, my brother would not have died. But I know that even now God will give you whatever you ask." Jesus said to her, "Your brother will rise again." Martha answered, "I know he will rise again in the resurrection at the last day." Jesus said to her, "I am the resurrection and the life. The one who believes in me will live, even though they die; and whoever lives by believing in me will never die. Do you believe this?" "Yes, Lord," she replied, "I believe that you are the Messiah, the Son of God, who is to come into the world.

— JOHN 11:20–27 (NIV)

As we continue dwelling in John 11, we will spend this week looking at Lazarus's sister, Martha, who had sent word to Jesus when Lazarus was sick. John 11:3 (NIV) states, "So the sisters sent word to Jesus, "Lord, the one you love is sick." She was proactive in sending news to Jesus that Lazarus was ill, yet Lazarus still died, and her heart was left to grieve the loss of her brother, alongside her sister, Mary. The word that was sent to Jesus was clear: her brother was sick.

I'm sure she was anticipating Jesus's arrival, but instead she found herself going through the process of laying her brother to rest. Jesus was late to her plea for help. When He arrived at the village gates, Lazarus was already wrapped in the grave clothes and tucked inside a dark tomb. Family and friends had been grieving his loss for at least four days when Jesus arrived. As we explore John 11 this week and look at the story of Martha, I invite you to put your focus into John 11:20–27.

Martha was a woman who approached Jesus with immediate and audacious faith. She was grieving the loss of her brother. The pain was real, and the loss was raw. I'm sure her frustration with Jesus was intense when she told him, "If you had been here, my brother would not have died" (John 11:21 NIV). I can just hear her tone full of anguish as she made this statement that sounds almost a question of "Where were you, Jesus?"

How many times have we questioned Jesus's

location in our hard times? How many times have we cried out, "God, where are You right now? God, if only You were here right now then, this would not be happening." We view God as our prevention mechanism, and when loss enters our space, so often we go to Him with blame of His lack of provision, and we become so sure that if only He'd have been there, this heartbreak would not have happened.

In my most heartbreaking of times, I have questioned Jesus's location in the struggle. It's okay to question and to run to Him full speed and start asking the hardest and heaviest of questions. I think we need to ask the questions so we can get an answer. Martha got her answer to the statement. "Jesus said to her, 'I am the resurrection and the life. The one who believes in me will live, even though they die; and whoever lives by believing in me will never die. Do you believe this?'" (John 11:25–26 NIV).

Sometimes I think all our hardest questions or statements to God are answered with this statement made by Jesus, the inquiry that He asked Martha shortly after her accusatory statement to Him. Jesus is always the answer to our heartbreak. He isn't the reason for it, but He is the answer.

We all face heartache. If you are facing it right

now or if it happens in the future, I want you to do three things:

1. I want you to make the statements and ask the hard questions to God if you have to. Start communicating to God even with an anguished tone. Cry out to Him. Yell if you have to. Just meet with Him.
2. I want you to remember that He is the only answer to your heartbreak. Look at the verse we just went over. It starts with "I am." There is your answer, sister. There will never be a question or statement that implies a question that He can't reply with "I am."
   a. "God, I am scared. If You had only been here, I wouldn't be sitting here fearful of losing my children." Jesus replies in John 10, "I am the good shepherd." He is the good shepherd, and you and your child are in His flock. He cares for and sees His flock. You are in this flock, and you and your child belong to Him.
   b. "God, I am so depressed. I just don't know how I am ever going to get out of this dark place of doubt as I watch my children struggle." Jesus answers in John 8: 12, "I am the light of the world. Whoever follows me will never walk in darkness, but will have the light of life."

On your own, your path may seem dark, but Jesus is answering you in this scripture. He's telling you three things:

a. Sometimes our ways and direction lead to darkness, but the direction of Jesus is always out of darkness. Follow Him. Let Jesus be your guide. He knows the way.

b. His path isn't dark.

c. He will light up your path and lead you to life every time.

I always asked the wrong questions. Instead of asking "Where are you, God?" I should have been asking, "God, my daughters have Joubert syndrome. It's terrifying. It has added so much trouble to our lives, but You are bigger than even this. So here we are stuck in the trenches of this syndrome. I don't need to know where You were when this happened because I trust You were right there next to me. What I need to know is this: how are You going to take this situation and use it for Your glory?" The diagnosis bound to your child stands no chance against the Great I Am.

3. It's your turn to answer a question. The answer to Martha's question may have started with "I am," but it ended with "Do you believe this?" Regardless of the pain, do

you still believe that Jesus is who He says He is? Do you believe that He is the Great I Am? And do you believe that He can take a dark path and light it up so bright that you need sunglasses? Do you believe that He can take the impossible and make it possible? Do you believe that He can make the lame walk? Do you believe He can raise the dead? Do you believe that even if He doesn't take away your child's diagnosis, He has plans to give your child a hope and future? Do you believe in the wine when all you see is the water? Do you believe that He can take what you see as a glass of water and turn it into something much greater?

Do you believe Romans 8:28 when we are told that God works for the good of those who love Him, who have been called according to His purpose? Daughters of the True King, listen to me. You don't have to see the wine to believe. You just have to give Him your water and believe in His hands. His hands might not perform the miracles you want, but trust in who He says He is, and you might just find yourselves drinking the best wine you've ever tasted.

Prayer

Lord Jesus, thank You for being in all our moments, even when we don't see You. Thank You for loving our children and trusting us to see the wine when the world would only see the water. I ask that our hearts and eyes would be open to Your goodness and that we could just delight in Your glory. Our journeys are hard, we are tired, our hearts fill with anguish from time to time, and we need You to answer us in our distress, God. We need to cling to Your promises, Lord. Please be with us this week, Lord. In Jesus's name. Amen.

Reflection Questions

What have you cried out to Jesus about in your journey?

_____

_____

_____

_____

_____

Have you ever asked where Jesus was in your times of grief?

_____

_____

_____

_____

_____

What comes to your mind when Jesus answers
Martha with "I am"?

_____

_____

_____

_____

_____

When you ask Jesus questions, do you take the time
to listen for His reply?

_____

_____

_____

_____

Do you believe Jesus is who He says He is, even
when His timing isn't in alignment with yours?

_____

_____

_____

_____

Treasures of the Week (Notes)

As you go through this week, let's be women who see the wine in our cup of water and promises in our heartbreak. Let's approach God's throne audaciously, like Martha with questions, and take the time to hear Him answer. And then let's write down what He tells us.

_____

_____

_____

_____

_____

_____

_____

_____

_____

Week 4

Mary: The Sister That Stayed

On his arrival, Jesus found that Lazarus had already been in the tomb for four days. Now Bethany was less than two miles from Jerusalem, and many Jews had come to Martha and Mary to comfort them in the loss of their brother. When Martha heard that Jesus was coming, she went out to meet him, but Mary stayed at home.

—JOHN 11:17–20 (NIV)

Last week we looked at one of Lazarus's sisters, Martha. We were encouraged by her audacious pursuit to meet Jesus upon His arrival in a time of grief and loss. This week we are going to look at Lazarus's other sister, Mary. She was one of the sisters mentioned in John 11:3 that sent word to Jesus of her brother's sickness. We know she was also in the same house of grief as her sister, Martha, after their brother died.

When Jesus arrived in her town she responded differently than Martha. Mary stayed home. Ladies, close your eyes for a second. Picture yourself in grief. Do you run or stay? Do you meet Jesus at the gates of your town, like Martha, or do you stay in the house, like Mary?

I always wanted to be a Martha. The way she approaches Jesus in hard times inspires me to the fullest. I got so caught up in wanting to be a Martha that I lost sight of the beauty in Mary's journey. Comparison does that. It's a thief of joy and an eliminator of sight. Comparison deceives us into thinking we aren't enough.

I wanted to be like Martha, but when God created me, He had a different vision in mind. My heart was structured differently, and in many ways, God created me to process pain similar to Mary. I want to speak to all you Marys out there who stay at home in the pain when you have the choice to run to Jesus.

Now we don't know why Mary stayed home. It could have been customary in those times that she stay with the people who came to mourn her brother or offer support. Maybe she knew that Martha was going to get Jesus, so she thought it was best for her presence to remain at home. Or perhaps she was just too heartbroken to move or knew the power in the Messiah's hands but was too heartbroken to think of the possibility that her brother wasn't worth Jesus rushing back before her brother died. Maybe Mary was questioning her worth because certainly if she were worth more, then Jesus would have returned earlier. We aren't sure why she stayed home. We just know that she did.

When my girls were diagnosed, I stayed. I was a Mary. It wasn't because I doubted God. It was because accepting who He is hurt too much. Accepting that He had the power but was choosing not to use it to take away the diagnosis just paralyzed me. I wanted to move, to run to Jesus full speed, but I couldn't. My place was at home, stuck in the mud of heartache. I entered a dark room with God, just Him and me. Every day we just sat in this dark room, and I would say, "God, I can't talk to you right now, but I'm here."

I call it my dark room, but actually it was a grief-filled room. Leaving that room would mean I had to accept that God was choosing not to use His power in the way I wanted Him too. I saw on Facebook other special needs moms running to Jesus as their strength, and here I was, refusing to go to church and to say anything more than "Here I am, God, but I'm not talking."

All I can say about this is that even though I wasn't talking much, God still showed up. I may have not talked more than one sentence, but I still showed up. And together, God and I would sit in silence. You see, God isn't afraid of the silence. He takes us even in the silence.

If you are a Martha and this doesn't relate to you, I ask that you pray for your sisters that this does relate to. If you are a Mary, let's have a little more time together through some prayer. Let's find beauty in the space we are in because you were created with such careful detail that God doesn't expect you to be a Martha. He loves you as a Mary. He loves you as the beautiful and broken woman you are right now. He wants your heart, and even if it's broken, He cherishes it. He wants to restore, resurrect, recharge, and refuel you. He wants to show you that He is the Alpha and Omega, Beginning and End, Conqueror, and True King.

He wants you to witness victory in defeat and to light up your dark room. He wants you, and even if He has to come into your space because you choose to stay in the room of grief, He will meet with you there every single time.

Prayer

Heavenly Father, we love You and thank You for loving us in all spaces. Lord, today I just want to pray for all the Marys and Marthas out there, the women who charge to You in their pain and the ones who meet with You in their dark room in their pain. I ask that You would just brighten up every dark place the women in Holland find themselves in times of grief. I ask that Your presence would surround the women who are reading this, that they would just experience Your pursuing love this week. I ask that You would speak truth, hope, joy, and peace into the hearts that are dark with sadness. Lord, let us experience Your grace this week. Let's see You and hear You, even if it's in a dark room. We love You, Lord. In Jesus's name. Amen.

Reflection Questions

When you experience grief, do you relate to Martha or Mary?

_____

_____

_____

_____

_____

In times where heartbreak fills your heart, do you find yourself comparing yourself to others?

_____

_____

_____

_____

_____

Have you ever spent time in a dark room that is thick with grief? How did you get out? Or are you still there?

_____

_____

_____

_____

_____

How do you hear from God when you are experiencing loss?

_____

_____

_____

_____

When Jesus arrived in Bethany, Lazarus had been dead for four days. Martha and Mary were prompt in asking Jesus to come to save Lazarus before he died, but Jesus arrived later than what they desperately wanted. Although Jesus arrived later than they wanted, He was still able to answer their prayers in a mighty way. When has Jesus answered a prayer in your life, even after you thought it was too late?

_____

_____

_____

_____

_____

Treasures of the Week (Notes)

As your week ahead begins, let's keep notes on the treasures that God places in your hands this week. Sometimes in the silence we hear Him the loudest. I challenge you to sit silently with Him every morning this week for fifteen minutes. Set an alarm and ask God to speak to you. Wherever you are this week, I have full confidence that He wants to be with you and to speak to you.

Although Mary waited to run to Him, when she finally left the house, a whole community of people followed her. Your grief is a part of your story. Let's experience God's goodness this week. Let's write down what He tells us.

_____

_____

_____

_____

_____

_____

_____

_____

_____

_____

Week 5

Worth the Stop

Jesus said to her, "I am the resurrection and the life. The one who believes in me will live, even though they die; and whoever lives by believing in me will never die. Do you believe this?"

"Yes, Lord," she replied, "I believe that you are the Messiah, the Son of God, who is to come into the world."

After she had said this, she went back and called her sister Mary aside. "The Teacher is here," she said, "and is asking for you."

When Mary heard this, she got up quickly and went to him. Now Jesus had not yet entered the village, but was still at the place where Martha had met him. When the Jews who had been with Mary in the house, comforting her, noticed how quickly she got up and went out, they followed her, supposing she was going to the tomb to mourn there. When Mary reached the place where Jesus was and saw him, she fell at his feet and said,

"Lord, if you had been here, my brother would not have died."

— JOHN 11:25–32 (NIV)

Let's ask ourselves if we are a Mary or a Martha. I have totally accepted that there are seasons where we are called to be a Mary and there are seasons we are called to be a Martha. But in this moment, which one are you?

Last week I shared that when my girls were diagnosed, I spent two years as a Mary. I stayed at home in my grief rather than run to Jesus at my city gates. During this time, I was also alongside my good friend, Sharon, who was fighting for her life against pancreatic cancer.

For years, we were very close. She was older than I was, and although she was a good friend, I also thought of her as an older sister. She loved bringing me cookies, and we had plans of opening a bakery one day. We spoke almost daily. During this time, both of us had so much to be angry about that our conversations drifted from dreams of our bakery to the dreads of our reality.

We both felt gypped and went through the anticipatory grief cycle daily. I was grieving the possibility of losing my girls; she was grieving the possibility of losing her life. I will never forget one of the hardest conversations we had during this time. She promised me that should she lose her life to cancer, she would go to God on my behalf and plead for the girls to stay in my arms. And if God said no, then she would be the one in heaven to receive them and keep them in her arms until it was my time to go.

It was a hard conversation, but it gave both of us a little peace in that moment. It gave her peace in knowing there could be purpose in her death; it gave me peace to know that my beautiful friend loved me enough to even think about going to God's throne in heaven and begging for my girls to stay in my arms. It was almost as if God paused time for us to have this conversation and we were on this mission together.

Shortly after this conversation, though, we were back to reality. We were lost in our own sadness, confusion, and frustration that so many times we would just talk for hours about the weight we carried. We both remembered our conversation and the promise made, but we never mentioned it. The difference between her and I was that she carried her weight to Jesus and I just held onto mine.

Two nights before she died, she woke up. She had been sleeping multiple hours at a time up until that point, but as I was sitting next to her, she woke up. Her words were direct although her energy was low.

She looked at me and said, "Mattie, I haven't forgotten about our promise. I am going to heaven to plead with God for you to keep your girls, and if He says no, then I will be there to get them, and I will keep them until you come." She was dying yet had a fire in her heart for me.

She was running to Jesus in the middle of her pain, and she hadn't forgotten about me. She knew I was in a room so dark and I hadn't had words for God in years, but she ran anyway. And then she met me two nights before she died and had the words I needed to hear to be able to receive Him. She was my Martha.

That night changed my life. As I left her house, I began driving home and had to pull over onto the side of the road as tears flooded my face. I started praying, and for the first time in years, my heart poured out the words I hadn't been able to say. It was a moment I will never forget. I fell at His feet.

At the beginning of this story, we see Martha leave her sister in the middle of the heartbreak to meet Jesus. It must have been hard for her to step away from her sister during such a heart-wrenching time, but she did it anyway. She stayed true to who she was. Her pain didn't stop her from meeting Jesus, and neither did her sister. I admire this about Martha. She was determined to meet

Jesus as soon as she could, even though it meant leaving her sister.

If you look at scripture, you will see that Martha and Mary both met Jesus with the same statement of "Lord, if you had been here, my brother would not have died" (John 11:32 NIV). They were grieving the same loss and battling identical frustrations, and literally they had the same statement for Jesus. The difference is that Martha met Jesus and Mary stayed home, but let's not miss one of the biggest points here that Jesus showed me. After Martha spoke to Jesus, Martha went to get Mary.

Martha didn't turn her back on her sister and think of herself as holier because she ran to Jesus in pain while her sister didn't. She didn't forget about her sister who still sat at home. She didn't even rely on someone else to get her out of the house. Martha went back to the house to get Mary because Martha truly loved her sister. Martha knew that Jesus loved Mary. Martha knew that in this painful time, Mary needed Jesus.

Also notice that she calls Him "teacher." That is the way Mary would be able to receive Him. Before this moment, these two women had years of a relationship where Martha had learned the way in which Mary would open her heart to leaving their house and falling at His feet. She used the word *teacher* and extended an invitation. I wonder how many of us, when hurting, just need a reminder that Jesus wants to meet with us. It's too hard for us to get there on our own, so we just need a Martha sister to come remind us that we are wanted in His presence.

Jesus waited for Mary after Martha went to get her. Scripture tells us that Jesus was still at the spot Martha met with Him. Ladies, Jesus knew He was about to raise the dead. Power filled His hands, and He was about to do one of the biggest miracles of the New Testament, but He waited because Mary was worth it. You are worth it.

And let's also not let it be lost on us that even though Mary stayed home for a short time, she led a whole crowd full of people to Jesus. Even while Mary was choosing to stay in the house, relationships were all around her. People were comforting and watching her. When she got up quickly, they followed. Nothing is wasted. God uses every space He can for His glory and your good.

I never had the chance to tell Sharon "thank you" for all she did through this season of hardship. She showed up even though she had grief of her own to carry, and she ran to Jesus on my behalf. Sharon was my Martha, and every day I am so grateful for my sister in Christ who loved me enough to bring me out of my dark room and to the feet of Jesus in her last days.

God shared this with me, so I want to share it with you. If you are a Martha, you have a beautiful gift. You Marthas out there, know where to find Jesus in your pain. It's a treasurable attribute that God stored in your soul when He created you. What makes Martha so admirable to me is her willingness to meet Jesus and then bring her sister to Him. We don't know if Mary would have ever left that house if it weren't for Martha. Mary was worth the stop for her sister.

And to all you Marys out there, pray for your Marthas. When you don't have the words for Jesus about your situation, pray there will be a sister out there for you who does have the words to meet Him with. It's okay to stay in the house, but don't forget you are worth the stop and the wait. Jesus is waiting for you. He isn't going anywhere. He isn't afraid of your pain, and He isn't going to shame you for it. He is waiting, and when you are ready to go meet with Him, He will be there, ready to receive you with arms once nailed to a cross for you. He loves you, and He will wait until you are ready to fall at His feet.

Prayer

Dear Jesus, we are women who love and trust You. Although we don't always understand Your timing, we trust it. I ask that You would bless every woman who is crying out to You in their dark room. I ask that You would send Marthas to run with their pain to You, and Lord, I ask You would fill the Marthas with guidance of how they can go to their sisters with words that would be received. Lord, I ask we would all surrender our hurt to You and fall at Your feet. Let us be women who stop for each other. Let us be women who invite sisters to Your feet. Jesus, I ask we would never forget that You are for us, not against us. May we walk with You and run toward You. Let's be women who chase Your garment, even in our pain. In Jesus's precious name. Amen.

Reflection Questions

Who are the Marthas in your life who stop for you? Who are the Marys you need to stop for?

_____

_____

_____

_____

_____

When in your journey have you experienced being worth the stop and wait?

_____

_____

_____

_____

_____

Have you ever felt that going to Jesus in your pain
was too hard? Would an invitation and a reminder
that you were wanted in His presence have made
this easier for you?

_____

_____

_____

_____

Martha called her sister out of the house shortly
before Jesus called Lazarus out of a tomb. Being
committed to Jesus is being committed to others
and letting others be committed to you. Is there
someone that Jesus needs you to commit to?

_____

_____

_____

_____

What pain, challenges, or hardships are you facing
right now? How can Jesus show you this week that
you are worth His stop?

_____
_____
_____
_____
_____

Treasures of the Week (Notes)

Section 1 is complete. We have been running to God's throne the past five weeks with burdens and placing them in His hands. How has He been blessing you? What has He been saying to you? Who has He been placing on your heart to help carry the burdens in this journey? You aren't alone in this, sister. We are in this together. As always, I pray you fill the spaces below about your week and write down all the ways you are experiencing Him.

_____
_____
_____
_____
_____
_____
_____
_____
_____

Section 2

In section 2, we will spend three weeks reflecting on obstacles we face with special needs children. We will discuss the reality of climbing the highest of mountains, putting one foot in front of the other when the rain comes and covers us in a downpour, and maintaining the determination it takes to keep moving when discouragement creeps in to stop us.

What if we were anointed, appointed, and equipped for every mountain we climbed and all the steps we take? What if we serve a God who loves our kids so much that He equipped us to be their parents with a purpose? What if Goliath is small to the giants we face? What if I told you to check your pockets because God already filled them with stones and a slingshot that won't miss?

Let's get to climbing and stepping. Let's remember we were anointed and appointed for our journeys and God will equip us every time for all we need to live a victorious life!

#HIGHALTITUDES
#THEJOYSTEP
#ANNOINTED/APPOINTED/EQUIPPED

Who made the great lights—
His love endures forever.
the sun to govern the day,
His love endures forever.
the moon and stars to govern the night;
His love endures forever.

— PSALM 136:7–9 (NIV)

Week 6

High Altitudes

Even to your old age and gray hairs I am he, I am
he who will sustain you. I have made you and I will
carry you; I will sustain you and I will rescue you.

— ISAIAH 46:4 (NIV)

Have you ever wanted to give up? Right now, I want to. I have been working with my daughter for three years on potty training. What most programs promise to be accomplished in three days of chaos has now extended to three years— three years of different programs; potty charts; unlimited candy and praise; cleaning up messes off the floor; watching my daughter not understand that her potty goes in the toilet, not in her pants; waking up with hopes of today being the day it just clicks; and going to bed disappointed and angry that it's not clicking.

This past year has been the worst because where anger lingers fear also follows—fear of this being a milestone we never conquer, her never being able to be in tune with her body, her never making friends who accept this flaw, and her future being poopy. How can she ever get sleepover and camping experiences? How can she ever be able to get a job or get through a public school with this constantly happening? What does this look like for my future?

I am reminded in this season that this has always been our normal, waiting for milestones to be conquered and working for years for what comes easy to others. On top of being desperate for these milestones, I also have to shut down the fears that most people never have to consider, stopping the enemy's tactics to steal my joy and destroy my hope. What some see as a milestone that comes at its normal time, I see it as a mountain that I climb and climb and climb without a view of the top in sight. And those times I do get to the top, I see in the distance the next milestone mountain that needs to be climbed.

Where's the pause? Where is the freedom in knowing that life will just continue and that my kids and I will land at the next milestone? See, those are not our lives. We are women who leave one milestone and feel the pressure to run our kids to the next one because we are already so far behind in the game. This constant milestone mountain climbing has left me weary, fearful of the present and the future. The mountain I am climbing now has brought me to a place of exhaustion.

I was sitting at the dinner table talking to God about my distress in this potty-training season that has now lasted three years. "God, who in scripture can I relate to? God, I need to read about a parent who didn't give up on their children when the battles are raging. I need someone in scripture who can bring me encouragement to keep going even though this potty training is messy. God, who in scripture do I need to lean into?"

God whispered back immediately, "Me."

Can I just say that I love when Abba God speaks? He speaks, and mountains move. He speaks, and the earth is formed. He speaks, and winds calm. He speaks in a battle, and victory is mine. He speaks in a whisper, and the rest of my life listens. He never leaves in our messes. He never walks away from our mountains. He tells me that I can do all things through Him and I can tell this mountain in front of me to move in Jesus's name and it will.

It may not move to the place I want it to or at the time I tell it to move, but it will move. As you wait for the mountains to move and as you seek God's voice, can I encourage you to do something I have found helpful to do in the waiting? I make a list of all the mountains God has moved in my life thus far. I reflect on it and pray through the list, thanking God for His faithfulness in my life. Then I start a new list that I keep by my bed.

Every night I ask God to show me the ways He's been faithful in my day. My list usually consists of, "Thank You, God, for protecting our family as we drove to our appointments," "Thank You, God, for providing food for our family throughout the day," and "Thank You, God, for surrounding my kids with Your love in all their moments today."

Focusing on the lists of God's faithfulness of the past and the present ways He is being faithful equips my heart with the hope I need to expect the faithfulness of God to move the mountains ahead of me. The posture of my heart shifts from being discouraged to being excited, ready, and expectant of God's faithful deliverance ahead.

I have found it so beautiful that when I asked God whom He wanted me to lean into from scripture, who in scripture I could relate to, He said, "Me." Of course it was Him. You see, milestone mountains are always going to be in front of my sweet girls. When we climb one mountain, there will be a bigger one behind it. I will be a mom who always climbs, who always has higher altitudes to travel. With that comes many times where I will want to give up. It takes blood, sweat, and tears to climb a mountain. Mountains will face everyone in this world.

For me, the mountains I face are actually my child's. God said "Me" because before Hannah and Elaina were mine, they were His. If God is my father, He is their father too. This means He too is a dad to special needs children. All the promises He made to us, He makes to our children as well.

God sees your mountain. He sees mine right now. This week I am going to rely on His promise in Isaiah. I'm going to claim it for you and me too. My mountain is big, and I don't know how to conquer this one. What I do know is that through the blood, sweat, and tears, God will sustain me. Those times when I want to give up, He will carry me. When I want to give up because I have no hope, He will rescue me. Our God sustains, carries, and rescues. It may take us longer, our trip may be lonely at times, pressure (which always changes at high altitudes) may creep in, and fear may intensify, but God made us for this. He chose us for the little people we climb for, and in His name, we will continue climbing. Even if we spend the rest of our lives climbing, He will stay true to the promise of always sustaining, carrying, and rescuing, and with that promise, there will never be a mountain we can't climb.

Prayer

Heavenly Father, we are climbers for Your children. Thank You for always sustaining, carrying, and rescuing us. Lord, let us always be able to admire the view from the tops of the mountains we climb. Remind us that You chose us to be the parents of the kids we climb for, and let us never forget that You climb for them also. You were their daddy first, and we are grateful that when we can't go another step, You promise to carry us. We love You, Lord. Amen.

Reflection Questions

What milestone mountain are you climbing?

_____

_____

_____

_____

_____

Do you experience the constant pressure of climbing mountains with no pause?

_____

_____

_____

_____

_____

When have you experienced God carrying you up a milestone mountain? When have you asked God to move a mountain out of your way and He has?

_____

_____

_____

_____

_____

What has been the hardest mountain to climb thus far, and how beautiful was the view when you reached the top?

_____

_____

_____

_____

_____

What advice would you give another mom who is climbing a milestone mountain right now that seems impossible to climb?

_____

_____

_____

_____

_____

Treasures of the Week (Notes)

Week six is underway! Whoop whoop! Sisters, we
are doing this. Mountains are no joke, but neither is
our God. Keep notes this week on how God shows
up to carry, sustain, and rescue you as you continue
to climb. Also, what mountains are you asking God
to move this week?

_____

_____

_____

_____

_____

_____

_____

_____

_____

_____

Week 7

The Joy Step

May the LORD repay you for what you have done. May you be richly rewarded by the LORD, the God of Israel, under whose wings you have come to take refuge.

— RUTH 2:12 (NIV)

A lot of special needs parenting is putting one foot in front of the other. It's a life of steps. Sometimes the steps are big; other times they are small. Occasionally we get gum stuck to the bottom of our shoes. And a few times we trip over our own two feet. But steps are always in front of us.

Ruth was a stepper. One day she was a bride; the next she was a widow. She could have had all these dreams of what could have been and the kids she could have raised, and then she was given a different reality. In many ways she was diagnosed to a life of loss, pain, and uncertainty the day her husband died.

It's easy for the circumstances of a diagnosis to command control over our lives. At least it was for me. It was easier to stand in the diagnosis of Joubert syndrome and watch it dictate our lives and future than it was to consider that God would have another plan for me to step into, one that would use the hardships we face as fuel for igniting the fire of our purpose. When I was standing in my girls' diagnosis, I was stuck in the mud. God didn't want me to be stuck. He wanted me to step out of the mud and into a joy-filled purpose.

When I was talking with God about writing about joy, He said, "Come walk with me." It was a rainy fall day. The thought of walking in the cold, rainy October weather was not appealing, but I needed to do it anyway because I've learned I can walk with Him through all the elements. I left the house, put my headphones in my ears, and started praying out loud for all the women who are living in a diagnosis rather than the joy of the Lord.

It was so freeing to pray for the women and myself that struggle in some of our steps. Our walk was coming to an end, and I started dreading the hill that led back up to our house. The wind was blowing, and the sky showed a promise that a downpour was moments away. I closed my eyes as I walked toward the hill and began singing "Beautiful Name" by Hillsong. At the end of the song, I opened my eyes and realized that I had just climbed the hill. Jesus so beautifully said, "This is joy."

Joy is climbing a hill in the windy rain but being so consumed by Jesus that, sister, you don't even see yourself climbing. Others will see you climbing the hill in the windy rain, but all you will see is Jesus. You will see Him in the steps, not the gum under your feet. No matter the size of the mountain, the downpour of rain, or amount of gum on your shoes, it's a daily walk with Jesus. It's a daily decision to lace up your shoes with the joy of the Holy Spirit and keep walking. It's closing your eyes to hardships so you can open them to His goodness. Joy is choosing to sing your way up the hill.

Ruth was burdened with the shoes of a widow, but she chose to start stepping. I'm sure many steps of her journey felt as if she were walking uphill and couldn't catch a breath. It was a time of unknowns and heartbreak for her. Ruth was encouraged to return to her homeland after her husband died, but instead she chose to stay with Naomi.

Naomi told Ruth that she should return to her parents and her old gods, but Ruth declared that

Naomi's God would now be her God and wherever Naomi went she would go too. She chose one God that would deliver versus many gods that were false because she trusted Naomi. On a side note, this is beautiful because it shows the beauty of trust. Ruth trusted Naomi's God because Ruth trusted Naomi. I believe that leading others to Christ starts with developing a relationship with others where trust is present.

Ruth committed to Naomi's God in her trial. She didn't need to know that her steps would take her to Boaz for her step with the Lord. I can imagine Ruth wept along the way, but she didn't stay stuck in the weeping. She continued to step into God's plan of redemption and restoration.

Ruth clung to her mother-in-law, and together they walked toward Bethlehem. When they arrived, Ruth had to work for the food she and her mother-in-law would eat. Ruth stepped up to serve her mother-in-law by gathering food from the fields. When Ruth could have crumbled, she chose to serve.

All these steps led to her future. The label of "widow" never left her. Marrying Boaz didn't take away the fact that she was first a widow, but in her walk with Naomi and the Lord, she developed a joy and trust that made her resilient. She stepped into the shoes of a widow and then the shoes of a provider as she served her mother-in-law and then the shoes of a wife to a good man named Boaz.

Together they would have a son, who would in turn have a son, who in turn would have a son, a king, a man after God's own heart named David, who would go on to write many of the Psalms. One of the passages from scripture that I cling to often is actually from the Book of Psalm, "When anxiety was great within me, your consolation brought me joy" (Psalm 94:19 NIV).

And then twenty-eight generations later, Jesus would be born down the same family line. Jesus, who was born in Bethlehem, the same town Ruth stepped to, would say, "As the Father has loved me, so have I loved you. Now remain in my love. If you keep my commands, you will remain in my love, just as I have kept my Father's commands and remain in his love. I have told you this so that my joy may be in you and that your joy may be complete" (John 15:9–11 NIV).

Ruth was a woman who stepped into the unknown and stepped up to serve when things were hard. Joy was developed in every step. Her broken story was restored and not just a little but to the full extent. Her commitment to stepping for the Lord led to the birth of King David as well as Jesus. Let's be women who step in and step up when things are hard, remaining in God's love so we can experience the joy that is promised to us.

Prayer

Lord Jesus, we love You and are so grateful for the joy You place in our journeys. I ask that You would continue to lace our shoes with joy every morning, we would trust You in uncertainty, and we would stay committed to You in the unknown. Jesus, as we step in joy and step up to serve Your kids, I ask that You would replenish us and surround us with people who would serve us as well. Jesus, we need You in our journeys, and our hearts crave Your joy. Be with us in every step, Lord. In Jesus's name. Amen.

Reflection Questions

Have you ever felt stuck in your child's diagnosis?

_____

_____

_____

_____

_____

When it comes to your journey, when have you noticed that your shoes were laced with joy?

_____

_____

_____

_____

_____

Is joy something you have asked Jesus to fill your journey with?

_____

_____

_____

_____

When is a specific moment in your journey that you have experienced joy?

_____

_____

_____

_____

In what ways can you rely on the joy of the Lord to be your strength this next week?

_____

_____

_____

_____

_____

Treasures of the Week (Notes)

Uncertainty and unknowns fill our journeys. We constantly choose to step in and up for our children. God wants you to continue stepping toward His throne of truth this week. You matter to Him, and He wants joy to fill your steps.

If finding joy in your day is something you struggle with, I want you to know you are not alone. Sometimes we focus so much on what is going wrong that we are not able to see all that is going right. When I struggle with not having much joy, I have found that writing out a "joy log" is helpful. Every day when I wake up, I will jot down at least three things I am grateful for, and when I end my day, I will write down at least five things I was grateful for throughout the day. I have discovered that having gratitude unwraps the gift of joy that is sitting right in front of me. Let's keep on writing the ways God shows up for us this week. Let's keep stepping in this together, love!

_____

_____

_____

_____

_____

_____

_____

_____

_____

_____

Week 8

Anointed, Appointed, and Equipped

Read all of 1 Samuel 16 and ask God to prepare your heart. Then proceed to Psalm 23 (NIV).

> The LORD is my shepherd, I lack nothing. He makes me lie down in green pastures, he leads me beside quiet waters, he refreshes my soul. He guides me along the right paths for his name's sake. Even though I walk through the darkest valley, I will fear no evil, for you are with me; your rod and your staff, they comfort me. You prepare a table before me in the presence of my enemies. You anoint my head with oil; my cup overflows.

Surely your goodness and love will follow me all the days of my life, and I will dwell in the house of the LORD forever.

Have you ever wondered if you were chosen for the task of being a special needs mom? Is it something that our Father in heaven handpicked for us, or is it something that just happens to a random few? I wish I had the answer to this. I don't, but I do know that there will never be a time or season in your life that God isn't capable of using for your good and His glory.

When we think of David, we think of a few things:

- a fearless shepherd boy who killed Goliath with a single stone
- a man who committed adultery and murder and experienced the loss of a child
- a powerful king who reigned over Israel
- a king who wrote many of the psalms and was known to be a man after God's own heart

David was a descendent of Ruth, and in time through this family line, Jesus would be born.

I think about King David and see him as a man who did so much. I see him fearless, flawed, and used for God's kingdom over and over again. But God has shown me that before David killed Goliath, wore a crown, and wrote the psalms, David was sought out and anointed. 1 Samuel 16:13 (NIV) tells us, "From that day on the Spirit of the LORD came powerfully upon David." This moment happened before much of his journey ever started.

I am not King David. I fight giants every day of fear, shame, and comparison, but I don't even know the slightest thing about a slingshot. My husband tells me I'm the queen of our castle, but I'm not the king of Israel. I do know what it's like, though, to be prepared for a journey I never saw myself in.

During my senior year of high school, God called me to be a nurse. I had signed up to work at Blossomland Learning Center, a school for children with moderate to severe special needs. When I first began this position as a student helper, I was very uncomfortable. I had signed up for this co-op program to make some extra money and have some time where I wasn't required to be in high school.

Stepping into this uncomfortable position led me to my purpose. What started as a job quickly turned into a love, passion, and calling. Within a couple of weeks of working at this school, I knew that I wanted to be a nurse and to spend the rest of my life helping those in need. As I went through the rest of my senior year, I developed such a bond with the students I served that I didn't want to leave them. I cried as I walked to my car on the last day, and even now, eleven years later, I get teary-eyed as I think of them. Those kids touched my heart and changed my life. I even thought of each of them before every nursing exam in college.

I was a newlywed when I started working nights, like most nurses do right after college graduation, and within a few short months, I was pregnant. My little girl Hannah was born, and I had a million dreams of what motherhood was going to be. The dreams I had for her seemed to be put on hold when I started noticing that Hannah's eye movements were abnormal and her development was delayed. Hannah was not able to track objects, and all of her milestones were lagging behind. The doctor informed us at Hannah's year-old checkup that Hannah had ocular motor apraxia and would need an MRI. Within a week of her MRI, she had a diagnosis, macrocerebellum.

Macrocerebellum required a specialist, as there is very little information on it and only a small number of known cases. The doctors couldn't figure out what was causing it at first, but they were sure our future would not be the one I had planned. I was also pregnant at the time with our second daughter, and the fear of the future was smoldering us out of joy.

My second daughter was born six months after Hannah was diagnosed. Her life began, and due to the significant delays we began to notice, an MRI was ordered around her first birthday. Joubert syndrome was the diagnosis we received, a syndrome with a high prevalence of liver and kidney disease. It only affects around one in eighty thousand to one in one hundred thousand kids in the world. It is typically diagnosed with an MRI because doctors are able to see the abnormal development of the brainstem and cerebellar vermis. Joubert syndrome causes cognitive, speech, and every other kind of delay imaginable. Many kids have lost their lives fighting the vicious diseases that often accompany Joubert syndrome.

After the diagnosis of my youngest daughter, Elaina, they checked my oldest daughter as well, and she had it too. Elaina's diagnosis led to us figuring out that Joubert syndrome was actually the syndrome that could have been causing the macrocerebellum in Hannah. The day their diagnoses came in was a day my whole life stopped, and I was put into another world I couldn't possibly imagine. My schedule was now filled with doctors' and therapy appointments and trips to the East Coast to see specialists who were capable of treating our girls.

Had I equipped myself for this journey? Absolutely not. How can any pregnant mom equip herself for this or even imagine it? I wasn't able to equip myself, to say the least, but I was anointed and appointed for it. My time at Blossomland put a love in my heart for children with special needs. My knowledge in nursing school prepared my mind to be able to understand all the medical lingo that would be thrown at me. The Holy Spirit had called me to a profession for the children I would be given four years before I even had my daughter Hannah. God prepared my heart and career ahead of time for our precious daughters.

It wasn't until I was facing the giant of Joubert syndrome that I realized how equipped I really was. I may not use a slingshot, but God equipped me with support, the right doctors, and direction at each moment of need. We serve a God that prepares and equips us. He prepared David the day He had Samuel anoint him, and then He equipped him with courage and confidence when the time came to take down Goliath.

Let's ask God to show us what areas in our lives He prepared for us before we received the beautiful children we did. For me, it was a nursing degree, but for you, maybe it's an abundance of patience, a person He brought into your life ahead of time to hold your hand through the trials of parenthood, or a marriage that is strong and steady for all the storms that come. Remind yourself that God didn't send this diagnosis to your child, but He did choose you to stand up to it. He did prepare you in some way for the giants you will face, and I trust that when the giants come taunting, He will equip you to slay them.

Psalm 23 is a verse that I have clung to in our journey. It supports the delightful truth that our God is a provider and an equipper. He equips us with all we need for all we face ahead. As you read through this scripture, ask God to illuminate the areas that you need to write on the tablet of your heart. I un-layered these verses and pray they meet you where you are today and encourage and equip you in your days ahead!

> "The Lord is my shepherd, I lack nothing."

Sometimes you may feel that you can't have a normal mom experience, but sister, I promise if you let the Lord lead you and be your shepherd, you will lack nothing. He supplies us in full!

> "He makes me lie down in green pastures, he leads me beside quiet waters."

He supplies us with rest and beauty. Green pastures are a place of growth, and being a special needs mom is a journey that is full of growth. God wants you to lie down and rest as growth continues to happen all around you. How gorgeous is a quiet stream? He knows we experience enough raging waters, and He is waiting to take your hand and lead you to quiet waters filled with a view.

"He refreshes my soul. He guides me along the right paths for his name's sake."

Ladies, we have a God that refreshes our souls. He doesn't make our hearts weary; He takes our weariness and replenishes us. He does guide us along the right paths. We don't have to figure out our whole life plans with doctors and therapists. We just have to trust that He will guide us. He guides my family, and I trust He is excited to take your hand and guide your family too because no matter the diagnosis, He will use it for His glory.

"Even though I walk through the darkest valley, I will fear no evil, for you are with me; your rod and your staff, they comfort me."

Why can't we run through the darkest valley? Why do we walk? This is another question I don't know the answer to, but I do know this: God is in that valley, and He has a rod and staff to protect you. I know that He treasures you and He surrounds His treasure with His mighty hands that save. I don't know your valley, but I know my God, and I know your valley isn't so dark that He can't light it up and comfort you the entire time.

> "You prepare a table before me in the presence of my enemies. You anoint my head with oil; my cup overflows."

Facing the enemy is inevitable. Moses had to face Pharaoh, David faced Goliath, and Jesus even came face-to-face with Satan in the wilderness. This scripture from Psalm 23 tells us that God prepares the table. He goes ahead of us to prepare the place we will sit face-to-face with our enemy. This scripture also tells us that when the time comes to sit down with our enemy, our cup will overflow.

Moses's cup overflowed with victory as he walked the Israelites out of Egypt, David's cup overflowed with victory as Goliath fell to the ground, and Jesus's cup overflowed with victory as He overcame an array of temptations when He faced Satan in the wilderness. All these instances are different but share the same concept: the enemies were forced to see the power of God as their opponent's cups overflowed with victory.

When I was engaged to be married, I was told that I wasn't of the Lord and God would never bless my marriage. This individual I craved belonging from always seemed to look for opportunities to remind me that I would never be good enough for her love. After our girls were diagnosed, I recall hearing these words ring in my ears again. I remember thinking, *Maybe she's right, or at least she gets to think she's right.*

I became super bitter that God allowed us to have hardships to face under her radar, and I truly believed it was a joy for her to think God really didn't bless our marriage by giving us children with disabilities. I told this individual and a few others about the importance of genetic screening as they could all be associated with the same genetic mutation. One person said, "Oh, this would never happen to me."

I was humiliated and angry with God. Why had He allowed these people to believe my daughters' diagnosis was a sign that He didn't bless our marriage? Why was I left with daughters who would struggle, not to mention easily face life-threatening diseases associated with their syndrome? Why would God allow this group of individuals to always be in a position where they could believe they were better than I was and that God's heart didn't want me just as their own hearts never wanted me? Why was I put in such close proximity with people who would rather judge my daughters than love them?

All these questions controlled my mind space for a long time. It caused division between God and me. I spent time asking God many questions rather than seeing the truth right in front of me. One of the issues was that I was seeking belonging from the wrong people. In fact, God needed me to see that although this group of people and I occasionally had to face each other at a table, I was never supposed to belong to them. I was only meant to face them.

They may have believed that I wasn't of the Lord and I didn't have a marriage blessed by God, which is why trials filled our lives, but Pharaoh also believed he was greater than the God Almighty who made demands through Moses. Goliath probably felt like facing David was a joke. Even Satan thought he was in a position higher than Jesus to try to manipulate Him.

Just because these enemies thought they were believing the truth doesn't mean they actually were. Pharaoh didn't stand a chance against God. He lost a son while trying. Goliath wasn't so mighty that stone didn't knock him over like a bowling pin, and Jesus would rather go hungry and thirsty than give in to the empty promises that Satan was trying to give Him. The individuals who believed my scenario was given to me because I wasn't of the Lord also believed a lie.

I was desperate to see that God was allowing my cup to overflow. This was shown to me at work one Sunday as I shared with a coworker about the heartbreak I endured knowing that people actually believed God caused my daughters' diagnosis on purpose as an affirmation that He hadn't blessed us.

My coworker looked at me confidently and said, "Girl, God's favor is all over your girls. I know that you may think these people think God's favor shines on them because they don't have to go through what you do, but I think you are wrong. Through your hardships, they are forced to see God's favor on your family over and over again. I think forever they will see God fighting your battles and your joy shining in the hills and valleys."

God prepared the table a long time ago for me to sit with them, but not because I was supposed to belong to them. It was so I could be a light to them. They would be forced time and time again to see God at the center of our lives, blessing each hardship we faced. A life with God is not a life without hardships; it's not even a life without enemies. A life with God is triumphing through your hardships and allowing your enemies to watch.

One more thing to consider: Psalm 23 also talks about God anointing our heads with oil. David's anointing story is beautiful. I wonder how David felt when all his brothers got to meet with Samuel to present a sacrifice while he had to stay back to tend to the sheep. He got to watch them go as they got to go and watch him stay. Jesse may have invited seven of his eight sons to the sacrifice, but God sought out the one who was not even there. He chose the one stuck in the fields, tending the sheep, and anointed him. God sees the uninvited and invites them every time.

Maybe you feel that your story keeps you from having a place at a table. Perhaps you feel unwanted, uninvited, or unworthy to sit beside people who have perfect-looking lives, or possibly you just feel like everyone you sit with can't comprehend the trials you face. No matter what, I believe we all face seasons in our lives when we feel we don't belong at a table, and we all face tables where we wish we were sitting somewhere else. Let's be reminded that we do have a table to sit at, not just any table, but a table that God Himself prepared for us. Let's lift our heads up and let the God of promises anoint us. I hope you never forget that you have a place and a promise. You have a God that wants your enemies to see His work in you, that no matter the diagnosis, fear, doubt, or hardship you endure, you have a place to sit. Lift your head up and take your seat. Your life will overflow with His goodness, and I can assure you that when your enemies see you, they will see Him.

"Surely your goodness and love will follow me all the days of my life, and I will dwell in the house of the LORD forever."

I know we worry a lot. We worry about the million things we can't control or a lot of things we just aren't sure about. Let's take a break from worrying about the things we are unsure of and claim what we know is true. God, we are sure that Your goodness and love will follow us all the days of our lives and that we will dwell in the house of the Lord forever.

When we think about our future, God reminds us of what is good and sure. I don't believe that God creates the giants we face, but I do believe He prepares us for them, and I am certain that when the time comes and the giants tower over us, taunting, He equips us to slay them. God didn't create Goliath to taunt Israel, but He did anoint David beforehand. And when the opportunity arose, God equipped David, and that giant fell.

I don't believe that God created the sickness or disease your child battles, but I do believe He prepared you for the journey, and I am certain that every battle you face, God will continue to equip you.

Prayer

God of angel armies, I come to You in Jesus's name and ask that You would be with all Your women in Holland. I ask that every giant of fear, shame, comparison, and doubt would be slayed in Jesus's name. I ask that You equip them daily for the battles they face and ignite their lives with victory as You give them their slingshots. God, Your daughters and their battles matter. I ask that You would show them this week how You have anointed and appointed them in this journey, and Lord, I ask that they would face their giants with courage and confidence in knowing that the God of angel armies is with them and equipping them. In Jesus's name I pray. Amen.

Reflection Questions

How has God anointed you for your journey?

_____
_____
_____
_____
_____

How has God appointed you for your journey?

_____

_____

_____

_____

_____

What giants do you face in your journey?

_____

_____

_____

_____

_____

How has God equipped you to slay these giants?

_____

_____

_____

_____

_____

What verse from Psalm 23 does God want you to meditate on and cling to?

_____

_____

_____

_____

_____

Treasures of the Truth (Notes)

I want you to know that when I think of a special needs mom, I think of a mom dressed in armor. We aren't just moms of kids with special needs. We are moms who climb the mountains and step into the unknown. We are moms who have been anointed for this climb, appointed with the kids we climb for, and equipped for all the giants we face along the way.

I want to invite you to run with me this week to God's throne. Let Him dress you for battle this week. Ask Him what your armor looks like. Ask Him to bring you victory as you fight the giants you face. You are wanted at my table, and the table I sit at is God's. Come, sister. Sit, write, and breathe. We are in this together. Now write all that God shares with you this week.

_____

_____

_____

_____

_____

_____

_____

_____

_____

_____

Section 3

Section 3 is four weeks of goodness and encouragement. The first week of section 3, we will ring into God's heavenly palace and be reminded that none of our prayers go unheard in our journeys. In the second and third week of section 3, we will look at two stories in scripture where healing was provided from the hands of Jesus. In week four of section 3, we will talk about the advocate hat we all wear as special needs moms and ways the Holy Spirit came to advocate for us and our children.

#RINGIN
#HOPELIKETHATPICKUPYOURMAT
#HIGHDEFINITION
#MOMOFMANYHATS

He determines the number of the stars and calls them each by name. Great is our Lord and mighty in power; his understanding has no limit.

—PSALM 147:4–5 (NIV)

Week 9

Ring In

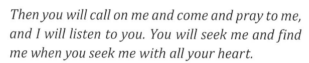

Then you will call on me and come and pray to me, and I will listen to you. You will seek me and find me when you seek me with all your heart.

— JEREMIAH 29:12–13 (NIV)

My youngest daughter, Elaina, loves talking to her dad before school. Every day she puts on her backpack and heads out the door before the bus comes. After she steps out onto the front porch, she reaches her hand up and presses our Ring doorbell. Within seconds, her dad begins to speak to her through the doorbell, and her face lights up with joy. They talk about her morning and what she had for lunch. He tells her to have a good day and says that he loves her. She tells him about the picture she colored and makes sure he can see what shoes she decided to wear for the day. They talk to each other for about five minutes, and then the bus comes, and she takes off to begin her afternoon adventure at school.

This routine is beautiful. It is truly special how my daughter has developed this daily daddy time on her own. You see, one day she was playing outside and rang our doorbell. When her dad's voice came through the doorbell, she was beyond excited. She realized that she can access her dad even when he isn't home if she just rings the doorbell. She can't see her dad, but he can see her, and she knows he's there. Even when he is miles away, she knows she has access to her daddy if she can just get to her doorbell.

What if we all carried a doorbell that when pushed, puts us in conversation with our heavenly Father? What if we had the confidence that my special little star, Elaina, has when she accesses her dad? What if we knew He would answer the minute we pressed in? Our heavenly Father can see us even when we can't always see Him and is always waiting to jump into connection with us and speak life into our day. He longs for us to press into Him. He wants to be in our whole day, not just our moments. He is found when we seek Him with our whole heart, and He always listens. Not a word you ever say to your Father in heaven will ever go unheard. He has a doorbell called "Heavenly Father, I come to you in

Jesus's name." Call on Him, come to Him, and pray to Him. He hears and sees you, and He's waiting to speak to you. All you have to do is ring.

Prayer

Dear God, Thank You for always being ready to receive us well and for cherishing us as Your children. Thank You for cherishing the children You placed in our arms. As we begin our week, I just ask that You would give us eyes to see You, ears to hear You, and hearts to receive You in full. I pray against any distractions that would try to steal our daily run to Your throne. I just ask that this week we would press into You, God, and that Your "ring" doorbell would be ringing off the hook from Your women in Holland. We love You, Jesus, and we want to experience You this week, Lord. In Jesus's name we pray. Amen.

Reflection Questions

God is fun and inviting. He is inviting all my sisters in Holland to ring in this week. He is going to hear you and to speak to you. We are going to ring in to Him this week. For the next five days, I encourage you answer one of the questions each day.

What's the first Christian song that comes to mind? I want you to go somewhere quiet—I know that is hard to find, but let's try—and play that song. Before you press play, though, I want you to ask God to speak to you as the song plays. Tell Him that when He hears the music start, it is you ringing into His throne. Tell Him you are dialing in and that your ears are open and ready to receive Him. Ring in, girl. I know what He speaks will be the best music to your ears! Maybe it's a vision, verse, or lyrics that your heart needs to cling to. What did He say or show you?

_____

_____

_____

_____

_____

Today will be fun. Thank you for trusting me and for trusting God to speak into your week. Okay, let's ring in. Where's your Bible? We need that, as today it will be our ring in to His throne. Let's close our eyes and pray that God would lead us in scripture. Follow these steps:

1. Commit to the doorbell. When you open your Bible and eyes, commit to hearing God speak to you.

2. Press the button. Close your eyes and start talking to Jesus. When you are ready, open your Bible to a random page.
3. Read His Word and hear His voice in the scriptures your eyes land on.

What did God share with you today?

_____

_____

_____

_____

_____

Sometimes my daughter invites me to speak to her dad with her. It's such a fun invitation to hear from my husband through our doorbell and be invited into such a sacred time. Today I invite you to invite a sister or spouse to ring in to God's throne with you. Ask them to pray for you just as you are. God loves togetherness, and He may actually have a message for both of you. When two or more are gathered, He is there. He will be with both of you. Trust Him and invite another into that space to hear Him talk. Ring in, sister! Ring in! What was the prayer space like as you rang in together?

_____

_____

_____

_____

_____

Go get your walking shoes on. The word *walk* is four letters, so it's fun that we do this one for question number four. Tell God that you are ringing in to His throne and you want to hear Him as you walk the earth He created. As you walk out of your home, claim that you are ringing in. He is excited to share with you as you walk in obedience to hear His voice. What did God share with you on your walk?

_____

_____

_____

_____

_____

Today your doorbell will be a pen and paper. I encourage you to write a letter to Jesus. As you begin your letter, tell Jesus you are ringing in. Write a letter to Him. Ask Him questions, and then close your eyes and let Him answer you with an image. Put the paper in your Bible. He will want to add to this through your journey. What is God showing you?

_____

_____

_____

_____

_____

Treasures of the Week (Notes)

Sisters, we have a God that answers, a God that wants us to press in and loves to speak with His children. As we continue to approach His throne, try to ring in through the day as well. Every parent longs to hear from their children throughout the day. Abba God is a good, good Father, and He wants to hear from His daughters. Take time to write it all down. He wants to use your story!

_____

_____

_____

_____

_____

_____

_____

_____

_____

Week 10

Hope Like That! Pick Up Your Mat!

Some time later, Jesus went up to Jerusalem for one of the Jewish festivals. Now there is in Jerusalem near the Sheep Gate a pool, which in Aramaic is called Bethesda and which is surrounded by five covered colonnades. Here a great number of disabled people used to lie—the blind, the lame, the paralyzed. One who was there had been an invalid for thirty-eight years. When Jesus saw him lying there and learned that he had been in this condition for a long time, he asked him, "Do you want to get well?"

"Sir," the invalid replied, "I have no one to help me into the pool when the water is stirred. While I am trying to get in, someone else goes down ahead of me."

Then Jesus said to him, "Get up! Pick up your mat and walk." At once the man was cured; he picked up his mat and walked.

The day on which this took place was a Sabbath, and so the Jewish leaders said to the man who had been healed, "It is the Sabbath; the law forbids you to carry your mat."

But he replied, "The man who made me well said to me, 'Pick up your mat and walk.'"

So they asked him, "Who is this fellow who told you to pick it up and walk?"

The man who was healed had no idea who it was, for Jesus had slipped away into the crowd that was there.

— JOHN 5:1–13 (NIV)

Hope comes in all shapes and sizes. Some hope to win the lottery, others hope for true love, a few hope for a miracle, and many hope to just make it out of bed in the morning. Hope is a place, an anchor, and a focus. It's a tunnel of vision of what my God can do when all that surrounds me says it can't be done. I've hoped for many things in our journey.

When I was reading through the book of John, I stopped at John 5, a passage that has many layers of God's goodness, but I want to stay focused on one specific part that I believe God wants us to cling to, hope. So let's dive right in.

In John 5, we see that Jesus went to a place where disabled people would gather, Bethesda. It was near a body of water that the Spirit of the Lord would stir from time to time, and the first person who could make it in the water would be healed.

As Jesus headed to this festival, He stopped at this location and approached a man who had been an invalid (disabled due to sickness) for thirty-eight years.

Jesus asked him if he wanted to get well. Okay, let's stop here for a second. Jesus saw this man lying on the ground, and that's the man He wanted to have a conversation with. Jesus is always intentional. We know from John 5:3 that many (disabled) people were in this place, yet Jesus approached this man, and I have to believe that it was because of the answer this man would give Jesus.

When Jesus asked the man if he wanted to get well, this man looked at him and said two things: he was alone, and every time he tried to get in the water that was being stirred, someone else got in ahead of him. Jesus could have approached any of the people in this place, yet He moved toward the one who was alone and left behind every time to watch someone else get the restoration he hoped for.

I can't imagine what that was like for this man—to have a disability that limited him to laying on the ground, to be alone, to watch everyone else get their healing moment, and to see God's miraculous powers restore the bodies of the people who left him behind to stay limited to the ground. He knew that someone would probably beat him to the water every time it stirred, but still he stayed anyway. This man had an anchored hope, one that kept him firmly in place to receive the restoration the Lord had prepared for him.

Have you ever had those moments? Those instants where your situation screams impossible? You see everyone else get their prayers answered, and you feel left behind. When my daughter turned two, she couldn't walk or talk. Therapists were showing me magazines so I could pick out a wheelchair, and doctors were telling me that she may never gain the core muscle strength to walk independently. I listened to their counsel, but I had a secure hope and a persisting perseverance. I started laying hands on her every day and praying out loud, "Lord, I ask that in Jesus's name Elaina would walk, talk, and praise your name." I prayed loudly and confidently that my daughter would get up and walk, talk, and praise the Lord that could heal her.

Shortly after her second birthday, I found an article about children with Down syndrome. Although my daughter does not have this condition, she does have low muscle tone, which is often found in children with Down syndrome. This article stated that putting children in a harness over a low-speed treadmill for eight minutes a day could lead to them walking sooner.

So we bought a pretty pink treadmill, and someone donated a harness to us. Every day we would put her on the treadmill and start the eight-minute timer. Her legs were often only moved by us until she gained the muscle strength to move them on her own.

My heart would break at the mall, playgroups, and just about anywhere I would see two-year-olds running up to their mamas with something to say. I felt left behind. I felt like my purpose was to stay stuck and celebrate the milestones of other kids while I watched my own child fall behind and be bound to the ground. I would lie down night after night, exhausted from the therapy on that treadmill. It was physically exhausting to carry her everywhere and put her in the harness every day. It was emotionally exhausting to enforce the treadmill every time since she cried through most of it. It would get weary at times laying hands on her to command she get up and walk, talk, and praise Jesus, as I would then watch her continue to lay on the ground. There were moments I wanted to quit, but I kept going because the hope in my heart was persistent. The hope and vision of her taking those first steps was more powerful than the heaviness of doubt that surrounded me.

I can see through the eyes of this man in John 5 because I know what it's like to be alone and to watch everyone else get their prayers answered. But then came Jesus. On the Sabbath, a day that healing was forbidden, on a day that this man must have least expected, Jesus walked up to him and healed him. It wasn't the way that this man had dreamed his healing moment would be. He had hoped to make it to the water and experience healing as the water stirred around him, but instead God saw this man and sent His Son, the living water, directly to him, and healing was restored to his bones.

I would love to take this even deeper. When Jesus healed this man and told him to stand up and pick up his mat, this man didn't even know who Jesus was. He was standing face-to-face with the Messiah, the Son of God, and didn't even recognize His face. Jesus sought out the one who wouldn't even recognize Him and healed him.

How many times in my life have I been face-to-face with the healing power of Jesus and not even noticed? How many times has He taken my hope and delivered more than I ask and I don't even recognize it? Ladies, God is a deliverer. He sees your unanswered prayers. I'm sure the people who passed by the disabled man in John 5 saw him as a man who didn't have a hope in this world.

They would be right. He didn't have a hope in this world, but he did have a hope in the God that created this world. And his faithful God brought healing directly to him. It wasn't the way he expected. It was even better.

Although my daughter's healing wasn't instant, it was beautiful. Jesus prepared all our steps to bring my daughter to her first steps. He led me to the perfect pink treadmill we purchased on sale for my sweet girl, and He just so happened to have a family donate a $7,000 harness to us the day our treadmill came. As He was building her muscle strength, He was also building her perseverance. So that way one day, when she would be able to walk, she would have the determination to run.

As I grew weary at times of laying hands on her and praying with no instant healing happening, I also grew in my patience. When I became weak from carrying her everywhere, God stepped in and showed me what it was like to be carried. What I hoped for was only a fraction of the whole picture God had planned.

My daughter doesn't just walk, talk, and praise Jesus's name. She runs, yells, and praises Jesus with her whole heart in the grocery aisle. It was more than I'd ever hoped for, and Jesus didn't want anything less.

I know all our stories are different. I know some mamas reading this may never see their children walk, talk, or praise Jesus's name. I know some mamas have had to endure decades of weariness.

If this is you, I want to tell you I see you and have hope for you. I believe that God wants to give you a bigger deliverance than you could ever imagine. It may not be the healing you pictured or the restoration you prayed for, but I promise that the God we serve is true to His promises. When He says in Jeremiah 29:11 (NIV), "for I know the plans I have for you, declares the Lord, plans to prosper you and not to harm you, plans to give you HOPE AND A FUTURE," I believe it.

Jesus has shown me time and time again that it's not how much hope you have. It's where you put it. My prayer is that even if you find yourself with only an ounce of hope, you place that ounce in the hands of the Father that multiplies and delivers. Let's have hope like that. Now pick up your mat!

Prayer

Lord God, I come to You in Jesus's name. I ask that You would be with every woman who is reading this. God, You are the safest place for our hope. You are a God that delivers. When we can't make it to the water, You bring the living water to us. You are a God that heals and restores. Lord, heal our past thoughts and restore our future. Take our hope and supply Your miracles to us in full. Lord, in your presence is where we will stay. We are Yours, and our hope will remain in You. We love You, Jesus. Amen.

Reflection Questions

What are you hoping for in life right now? Do you find it hard to place your hope in God's hands?

_____

_____

_____

_____

_____

Bethesda is a place where disabled people gathered in hope to receive healing. Where do you seek healing?

_____

_____

_____

_____

_____

Do you feel isolated in your times of suffering? Have you felt as if others walk past you in times of hardships without stopping to help carry you toward places of healing?

If so, can I apologize on their behalf? You were never meant to do this journey alone. I believe

God's heart is to have all of us surrounded by people who will bring us to healing waters or bring the healing waters to us. If you are someone who struggles with isolation, I want to invite you to write out a prayer and ask God to surround you with women who don't walk past you in pain but choose to stop for you and help you heal. Joining a church small group can be quite scary, but it would also be a great first step to meeting women and forming life-giving relationships. Small groups are also a great way for other women to learn how to stop for special needs moms and gain insightful perspectives on hardships they have not had to face.

_____

_____

_____

_____

_____

When is a time that you have come face-to-face with Jesus in your journey and not even recognized it was Him?

_____

_____

_____

_____

_____

What can you tell Jesus you want healed in your life this week? He is trustworthy, and you and your child are worth His stop.

_____

_____

_____

_____

_____

Treasures of the Week (Notes)

Bethesda is a place I think about often. It's a place where a man received a miracle in a way he wasn't expecting. I want to be a mama who waits in God's presence for Him to deliver more than I ever asked for. I want to be a mama who approaches His throne every day with hands of hope. He invites you; I invite you.

We are in this journey together. Let's be women who gather with two purposes, either to carry each other to the healing water or carry the healing water to the people. Jesus will always be the water we carry, and let's do it well. Let's secure our hope in Him this week. Take notes this week. If you have trouble trusting God and saying yes, I encourage you to ask Him to speak to you this week. Ask Him to remind you why He is trustworthy. You are loved.

Hope Like That! Pick Up Your Mat!

_____

_____

_____

_____

_____

_____

_____

_____

_____

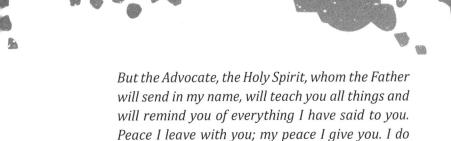

Week 11

Mom of Many Hats

But the Advocate, the Holy Spirit, whom the Father will send in my name, will teach you all things and will remind you of everything I have said to you. Peace I leave with you; my peace I give you. I do not give to you as the world gives. Do not let your hearts be troubled and do not be afraid.

— JOHN 14:26–27 (NIV)

Special needs mamas wear many hats. All of them are beautiful and unique and created with purpose. My hat drawer sometimes seems quite full, overflowing in fact. I have my sporty hat that I wear most days as I'm running around to find their homework and hurry to get them to their horseback riding lessons, taekwondo practice, and school on time. I have my painter's cap that I wear often as I creatively attempt to paint ways for them to experience all the same things their peers do. My hospital hat reads "Johns Hopkins," and I get to wear that one once a year as we go through our annual week of meeting with specialists and doctors, ultrasounds, and lab work. I wear a hat that reads "translator" most days as I have to translate the words my daughters are speaking because their speech is delayed and most people have a hard time understanding their communication. Sometimes I have to wear earmuffs to tune people out as they give me all their opinions on my situation that isn't theirs. Somedays I even have to wear the referee hat as my girls hash out their differences on the living room floor. The hat I want to talk about today, though, is the advocate hat, and I wear it almost daily.

My advocate hat is special and sacred to me as it was placed on my head when my oldest daughter, Hannah, was just fourteen months old. Although I wear the advocate hat with both of my girls, I want to talk for a little bit about my journey with my special little star, Hannah, and what it has been like to be her advocate. When I first started advocating for her, I thought that advocating was teaching others about her diagnosis. I thought that it was ensuring all the therapists were on the same page. When she was three, she used sign language because she didn't have the oral motor skills yet to begin talking. A lot of my advocating was teaching others the sign language we used so they could communicate with our little princess.

As Hannah got older, I found myself advocating for her in other ways. When I could see she was capable of doing something on her own but wanted me to do it, I would say no. It was hard to watch her struggle sometimes as we went on walks. Although she was able to walk at sixteen months old, she still had low muscle tone, and walking around the block at three years old would tire her out. About halfway in our walk, she would want me to pick her up and carry her. I knew, however, that finishing the walk would only make her stronger, and I wanted to be a part of her getting-stronger story, not her enabling story. A huge part of the advocate role became equipping and encouraging her to do all she can do.

Recently I have begun to advocate for Hannah by supporting her passions. Over the past six months she has developed a love for the environment. At first she didn't want us to use plastic straws because somebody at a restaurant informed her that plastic straws were killing sea turtles. Then Hannah went on a field trip to the landfill, and oh boy, did our dinner conversation get heated. She demanded we rewash all our trash and throw nothing out. She was yelling, and her face got beet red. She was passionate. She wanted us to begin recycling and to turn off the water when we were brushing our teeth.

As I was driving her to school the day after our heated dinner conversation, the Holy Spirit spoke to my heart. "Hannah has a gift for loving God's ground. She sees the worth in God's creation, and she wants to protect it." What a humbling moment this was for me, as I was able to experience the Holy Spirit advocating for Hannah.

The night before, I had watched Hannah yell and cry that we would not wash her pudding cup. I found it humorous, and to be honest, my husband and I laughed about it before bed. When the Holy Spirit met with me the next morning, it changed the whole situation. I was humbled and empowered in the same second.

You see, the Holy Spirit came to me on the behalf of the Father who knit Hannah in the womb with this gift, to see God's creation and want to protect it. She sees the trees and wants to see them flourish, not get cut down. She sees trash on the road and wants to pick it up. She sees sea turtles on TV and wants to save them all. Hannah sees our environment as a reflection of God's gift to us, and she wants to keep it clean and green.

I wasn't born with the gift Hannah has for

seeing the earth as she does, but I am so happy that the Lord sent the advocate, the Holy Spirit, to prompt me to help steward this gift rather than laugh at it. Now I own reusable straws and try not to leave the water running when I brush my teeth. I buy her books on the ocean so she can learn even more about the animals she is passionate about. I create opportunities for her to tell others about her passions, and I let her know that although I wasn't born with the same drive, I am so honored that she was so she can teach me.

Advocacy becomes our middle name when we become mothers. We strive to help our kids, and we learn all we can about the diagnoses they face so we can to provide them with all the resources they need to be successful. Many of us watch our kids struggle in school and with their peers. We work hard to explain their diagnoses and difficulties with others to ensure our kids have all the same opportunities and experiences as their classmates. We advocate with doctors on behalf of our kids' treatment plans, and we advocate at therapy sessions when our child just needs a break. We advocate at IEP meetings, and we even advocate for them on the playground at the park. We become creative for providing opportunities for them, and we develop a voice to speak up for them.

I believe special needs moms advocate on a

daily basis. I also believe that when God chose us and entrusted us with the children we received, He knew we would be able to advocate for them in the way they needed. He knew we would be their voice and that our love for them would fight for them in all settings.

I often think about the future and what will happen when I am no longer here on this earth to advocate for my girls. What will happen when I am not able to teach others about their needs or provide for them the way I do? Maybe you are a mom who thinks of this too, or perhaps you lie in bed at night and wonder how your kids' needs will be met when you leave this world.

When I entered into motherhood, someone told me the best thing I could ever do for my child is to teach them to care for themselves. I was given a different journey, one where I had to accept my daughters may never be able to live independently. I have also learned that it's okay to disagree with the advice given to me. My journey has taught me that teaching my kids to care for themselves isn't the best thing I can do. The best thing I can do as their mom is to ensure that they know they have identity, belonging, and purpose in Jesus Christ and to be confident that Jesus will never leave them and always provide for their every need. God has already shown me that He loves Hannah so much that He's willing to send the Holy Spirit to me to guide me in my interactions with her to ensure that I steward the gifts He's given her.

During this time with the Holy Spirit, it also showed me that God is a pursuing God and I need not worry about always being present to advocate for my girls. That solution was provided a long time ago. The Holy Spirit will continue advocating for my girls with others—future bosses, teachers, and even their friends. The Holy Spirit is with my girls even when I am not.

The Holy Spirit is with your kids too. It's the best gift, the best treasure, the best guide in our journeys. God created your child on purpose for a purpose. He chose you to be their mother. It was intentional. Let us be moms who call on the Holy Spirit to guide us in child-rearing, and let us be reminded that the Holy Spirit will never leave our kids. Our kids have an advocate for life, the Holy Spirit. We are just vessels, entrusted employees of God to be bonus advocates for them!

Prayer

Heavenly Father, we love You and are so grateful for You. Thank You for sending an advocate to us. Thank You for recognizing that we needed an advocate to remind us of Your promises. Lord, we wear many hats, and I ask that You would bless each of them. As we go through our week, I ask that You would advocate for us and our children, that You would remind us of Your promises and show us all the ways You have gifted our children. Show us how to advocate for our kids as their life is full of purpose for Your kingdom. I ask that You would send Your servants to help us on our journeys and that we would receive them well. In Jesus's name. Amen.

Reflection Questions

What hats do you wear that are unique to your journey?

_____

_____

_____

_____

What passions do your kids have? How could you see Jesus using those passions for His kingdom?

_____

_____

_____

_____

How can the Holy Spirit advocate for you this week?

_____

_____

_____

_____

How can the Holy Spirit advocate for your child/
children this week?

_____

_____

_____

_____

Close your eyes and spend some time with God.
You wear a lot of hats, but God wants to give you
a crown. You are His daughter, and He made you
with such purpose. Ask Him what your crown says.
Ask Him to reveal to you who He says you are. It's
one of the ways He can advocate for you right now,
to remind you who He says you are. What does
He say?

_____

_____

_____

_____

Treasures of the Week (Notes)

The week ahead is on its way. I know that the Holy Spirit is going to meet you many times throughout your week. As you approach God's throne this week, ask Him how you can advocate for your children this week. Ask Him to advocate for you. As always, write it down. There is so much purpose in writing down all that He shares with you this week.

_____

_____

_____

_____

_____

_____

_____

_____

_____

Week 12

High Definition (Fight for Your Sight)

They came to Bethsaida, and some people brought a blind man and begged Jesus to touch him. He took the blind man by the hand and led him outside the village. When he had spit on the man's eyes and put his hands on him, Jesus asked, "Do you see anything?" He looked up and said, "I see people; they look like trees walking around." Once more Jesus put his hands on the man's eyes. Then his eyes were opened, his sight was restored, and he saw everything clearly.

— MARK 8:22–25 (NIV)

The blind man in Mark 8:22 had no sight. Before Jesus met with him, he could not see the world with his eyes. The first verse in this passage tells us that when this man lacked sight, people with vision surrounded him. He was surrounded by people who could identify the way to Jesus and knew that this man was in need of Jesus to restore his sight. The people who surrounded this blind man were willing to take him to Jesus and beg for Jesus to touch him. Jesus received this man with no vision, and instead of walking the other way, he grabbed his hand and began to lead him outside of the village.

Sight didn't come to this man in that instance, but he chose to walk with Jesus anyway. The first time Jesus spit on this man's eyes and laid hands on him, his sight was not restored instantly, but he began to see. It was a process. He saw people even though they looked like trees. He was honest about it with Jesus. He told him that he was starting to see, but it still wasn't clear.

Jesus continued to pursue the healing of this man's vision. This blind man stayed and allowed Jesus to continue healing his sight. Jesus put His hands on this man's eyes once more, and His sight was restored. Scripture tells us this man saw everything clearly.

Have you ever had times in life where you weren't able to see? Times where you found yourself trying to focus your eyes on a situation that seemed blurry? Or what about times when you thought you saw a situation clearly, only to look back on it and realize you weren't seeing clearly at all?

Well, Disney+ had just launched, and I was so excited to watch some of my old favorite Disney shows with my girls. I turned on an old favorite show, *Lizzie McGuire*, and immediately noticed that the TV was blurry. It took a little while for my eyes to adjust to the low-definition composition. I had forgotten that I used to watch TV in low definition. My eyes have become almost spoiled when I watch TV these days with the high-definition settings that we have today. It really opened my eyes to the growth of our technology and the way my eyes have adapted to the growth. What I used to watch and think was clear is nothing compared to the clarity I see now when I watch TV.

As I was reflecting on the growth of technology and watching *Lizzie McGuire*, God spoke to me. He said, "Mattie, do you believe you used to think this was clear?" His question to me took me into deep thought. Sometimes I look back at situations and wonder how I didn't see all that I do now. I think about my journey with my youngest daughter. It's heartbreaking for me to say that for so long I would look at her and only see her diagnosis. On her beautiful face, I would see Joubert syndrome looking at me. I saw her in the lens of the false identity the enemy wanted me to see her through. I would look at her just to see and grieve all that she was not because of the diagnosis that was bound to her. It prevented me from seeing my precious girl clearly.

At that time, I thought I was seeing her clearly. It was black and white, right? This is what she will do; this is what she will never do. This is what the doctors say about her future, so this is what I must believe about her future. I was looking at my daughter in the wrong lens, and even though I thought I was seeing clearly, I wasn't seeing clearly at all.

Jesus found me in that place with no sight. I was at a church service where a pastor was talking about identity. During this service, Jesus took me by the hand and asked me to walk with Him. He had a lot to show me. He opened my heart to show me that I was letting Elaina's diagnosis define what I saw, but He needed to me to define her by what He saw.

As I am writing this today, I can picture God with His hands focusing my eyes as if He were focusing the lens of a nice, fancy camera. As I held His Son's hand, sight began to get clearer for me. I started to see my daughter through His lens, and my vision changed. When I saw my sweet little girl, I started to see the child God created—a little girl who loves to dance, pray, and ride horses. She has a joy that shines bright and a heart that loves to give. I saw her serving at the food pantry with giddiness and delight as she was able to be a part of a solution for others. I started to realize that my journey was one where I would need to fight for my sight and I needed to be surrounded by women who would fight for it too.

For so many years, I didn't have friends who had vision for my sweet Elaina, but after I began to see clearly, I started to pray for friends who see clearly too, those who can see my daughter as a daughter of the King, not a syndrome, friends who see her purpose when all I can see is her IEP scores.

I knew that in our journey there would be times that my vision could get compromised. I needed friends who would be able to recognize when I wasn't seeing clearly and take me to the only one who can restore my sight. I asked God to bring forth people who could always know the way to Jesus and would be willing to beg for my sight. Jesus took my hand, and every step with Him, I started to see more clearly. He surrounded me with women who have vision for my girls, women who see through the lens of God's promises versus the worldly view of their syndrome. God continues to focus my eyes every day to see Elaina the way He sees her. I've learned that the worldview is low definition, but God's view will always be the highest definition and the best clarity.

Jesus wants your hand, and He wants you to

have sight. I know that it's easy as a special needs mom to lose sight. We are frequently overwhelmed in our journeys, and the busyness alone can rob us of sight. Asking God to show us what He sees in our child is the first step. I had a conversation with God about the identity of Elaina, and He said, "She is my masterpiece. I made her in my image. A piece of the master is within her."

When God, the Master, designed Elaina, He placed a piece of Himself within her. He does this for all His kids. Just like our kids look like us, there is spiritual DNA in all God's children that reflect the image of God.

Asking God to send us friends who can see when we lose sight is an important next step. He wants you to see the beauty in your kids, the children He chose for you. Our God is a God of community. He would love the invitation to enter into your relationships and bring forth friends who can have sight for you when you can't see clearly. He wants you and others to see your kids as the masterpieces they are. He wants you to see the clear picture of the identity He spoke over them as He was designing them.

Ladies, your children are much more than their diagnoses. They are children of the King. He calls them chosen and beloved, and He set them apart and placed them in your arms. Their diagnoses don't give them their identities. God does.

I pray that all of us will have friends who can see when we can't and friends who take us to Jesus in those times when we think we are seeing clearly but in reality our sight is stuck in low pixels. I pray that together we can hold Jesus's hand and let Him lead us daily to give us sight for all He sees in our kids, that there would never be another moment where we let a diagnosis steal our vision for all that Jesus created our kids to be and all the many ways He will use them and their journeys.

Prayer

Heavenly Father, I ask that You would send support to each special needs family. I ask that You would surround all of Your daughters with people to see when their vision gets cloudy. Show us what You see when You look at our family and show us the many ways our children were born to shine in the authentic way they do. Empower us with Your vision, God. We love You, Lord. In Jesus's name. Amen.

Reflection Questions

Who in your life has vision when you lose your sight?

_____

_____

_____

_____

_____

When is a time in your life where you thought you were seeing something clearly but then look back and realize you weren't seeing clearly at all?

_____

_____

_____

_____

_____

When you look at your child, what do you see? Pray and ask God to show you what He sees when He looks at your child. What did He say?

_____

_____

_____

_____

_____

When you look at yourself, what do you see? Pray and ask God to show you what He sees. What does He say He sees when He looks at you?

_____

_____

_____

_____

_____

What is something that you struggle to see? What can God give you a vision on this week?

_____

_____

_____

_____

_____

Treasures of the Week (Notes)

Spend time this week asking God to heal your eyes so that every moment with Him you will see clearer. What details in your story have you not seen clear up to this point? How can you be a friend with vision for somebody who is seeing something in low pixels? Take notes on all that God is showing you this week.

High Definition (Fight for Your Sight)

_____

_____

_____

_____

_____

_____

_____

_____

_____

Section 4

As we enter section 4, the final section of this book, we are going to enter a storm in Matthew 14 and spend four weeks in verses 22–33. Each week we are going to reflect on the storms our children's diagnoses have brought into our lives and how we can develop an unwavering faith amid them. We are going to let our hair blow in the wind and step out onto the waves that come against our boat. Our hands will remain stretched out toward the one who's steady in the chaos.

Should we begin to sink, we will experience immediate rescue by the one we are walking to. The sky is going to get dark, the waves are going to get high, and the wind is going to blow, but we are going to have faithful feet and a fearless focus to get out of the boat and walk right through the windy, wavy weather! And we are going to show others in our boat (and the boats around us) that we can walk on the waves that can easily sink us!

#WINDYWEATHER
#WALKINGONWATER
#FEARLESSFOCUS
#FAITHFULFEET

Those who are wise will shine like the brightness of the heavens, and those who lead many to righteousness, like the stars for ever and ever

— DANIEL 12:3 (NIV)

Week 13

Windy Weather

Immediately Jesus made the disciples get into the boat and go on ahead of him to the other side, while he dismissed the crowd. After he had dismissed them, he went up on a mountainside by himself to pray. Later that night, he was there alone, and the boat was already a considerable distance from land, buffeted by the waves because the wind was against it.

Shortly before dawn Jesus went out to them, walking on the lake. When the disciples saw him walking on the lake, they were terrified. "It's a ghost," they said, and cried out in fear. But Jesus immediately said to them: "Take courage! It is I. Don't be afraid."

"Lord, if it's you," Peter replied, "tell me to come to you on the water."

"Come," he said.

Then Peter got down out of the boat, walked on the water and came toward Jesus. But when he

saw the wind, he was afraid and, beginning to sink, cried out, "Lord, save me!"

Immediately Jesus reached out his hand and caught him. "You of little faith," he said, "why did you doubt?"

And when they climbed into the boat, the wind died down. Then those who were in the boat worshiped him, saying, "Truly you are the Son of God."

— MATTHEW 14:22–33 (NIV)

As we begin this week, let's jump right in at the beginning. I want us to focus on the beginning of this passage this week.

> "Immediately Jesus made the disciples get into the boat and go on ahead of him to the other side, while he dismissed the crowd. After he had dismissed them, he went up on a mountainside by himself to pray. Later that night, he was there alone, and the boat was already a considerable distance from land, buffeted by the waves because the wind was against it" (Matthew 14:22–24 NIV).

Have you ever felt like Jesus sent you on your way, just to find yourself in a windstorm? In this passage, we see that Jesus tells His disciples to get in a boat while He would dismiss the crowds for them. They get into the boat just as they were asked, and after the day they had, I have to imagine they thought the boat was going to be a place of rest for them and that they would just mosey on over to the other side while their teacher dismissed the crowd. Piece of cake, right?

The disciples were obedient when Jesus told them to get in the boat. They listened and did just as He asked, right? So then why does verse 24 say "and the boat was already a considerable distance from land, buffeted by the waves because the wind was against it" (Matthew 14:24 NIV)? This boat was filled with men dedicated to preaching the gospel and bringing healing to the lands as they walked with the Messiah. They listened to Jesus when He asked them to get in the boat, and they trusted Him. So why then was the wind against their boat?

I remember when I was pregnant. Both times I was so careful. I didn't eat sushi, drink wine, or even listen to my music too loud. I prayed constantly over my little blessings. I wouldn't even touch caffeine, and I set schedules to make sure I didn't forget my vitamins. Ladies, I was super obedient to every pregnancy book I read and obedient to the doctors who were overseeing my care. I was obedient to the Lord and actively praying, yet after my girls were born, I found myself in a windstorm, not once but both times. How could this be? I did everything so right. Do you feel this way too?

God drew my attention to "because the wind was against it" because I needed to see that sometimes the wind can be against obedience. In fact, when you are obedient to the Lord, you will often find yourself in windstorms. He focused my eyes and heart on "because the wind was against it" because I needed to see that the wind was against the boat, not Jesus. Sometimes I think when the wind starts to blow, we think it must be something we did wrong, almost as if Jesus is trying to blow our boat away because we didn't do something the right way. We caused this, right? This diagnosis was something we did or didn't do. Our kids will suffer because we must have done something wrong.

Well, the disciples did as Jesus asked, and the wind still blew. And sisters, as the wind was blowing, Jesus was performing miracles all the way through it. Every single step on the water was a miracle. He didn't just perform one miracle on His walk out to them. Ladies, it was miracle after miracle. He was walking on the same waves that were rocking their boat. The disciples weren't able to see the first few miracle steps that Jesus began taking. They were far from the land that Jesus stepped off of, and it was nighttime.

They couldn't see the initial steps, but that doesn't mean Jesus wasn't walking or He hadn't started performing the miracles. Just because we don't see Him when the wind starts to blow doesn't mean He isn't on His way. He was performing miracles even when the disciples couldn't see it.

> Shortly before dawn Jesus went out to them, walking on the lake. When the disciples saw him walking on the lake, they were terrified. "It's a ghost," they said, and cried out in fear. But Jesus immediately said to them: "Take courage! It is I. Don't be afraid." (Matthew 14:25–27 NIV)

In this passage, we see that the disciples do see Him as He approaches their boat. The wind was blowing, the waves were high, and the sky was dark, but that didn't stop the disciples from seeing Jesus. They saw Him walking on the water.

I wish when the wind began to blow in my dark, windy waters, I would have been looking for Him. I wish I could have listened for His words, "Take courage! It is I. Don't be afraid." I wish that even when I didn't see Him, I would have trusted that

He was already stepping into the wind, walking toward me. Not even the wind and waves can stop Him from miracles.

Sisters, hear me. Jesus will always be above the waves. He will always be headed toward your boat, one miracle after the other. You may not see it yet, but you keep your eyes open. When the wind wants to scare you and the waves get high, I want you to declare that your Jesus walks on those waves and the wind doesn't stop Him from getting to you.

I will end on this note: Beloved, when the winds blow and waves buffet your boat, I want you to look for Him. He is on His way, and He wants you to take courage because He is coming. He is walking to you miracle step after miracle step. You are going to see Him and all His power in such a mighty way that the waves won't even scare you anymore because you will see Him walking on them. His power, strength, and purpose will always be greater than the winds that blow against your boat. And He will look at you and tell you in the middle of the windblown waters, "Do not be afraid."

Sister, the waves may be crashing into your boat, and the wind may be hitting you in the face, but Jesus is already stepping toward you, and nothing will stop Him from reaching your boat before dawn.

Prayer

Heavenly Father, thank You for this journey that we have been on together. I believe that each week we have covered thus far has prepared us for the next four weeks. We are listening and ready to look up. Lord, give us the discernment to see that the wind may be against us but You are for us. Jesus, give us the eyes and courage to see You when the wind hits our boat.

Lord, I ask that fear would leave our lives and peace would fill that place. We don't always have peaceful waters in our journeys, but God, I ask that you teach us to walk on the waters we find ourselves on. The first step is seeing You, Jesus. Let us see You, even in the wind, waves, and dark. In Jesus's name. Amen.

Reflection Questions

Have you ever been told or believed that you caused the diagnosis that your child has?

_____

_____

_____

_____

_____

When the wind is against your boat, do you recognize that it's the wind, not Jesus, against your boat?

_____

_____

_____

_____

_____

In those times where you have found yourself in the middle of the windy, wavy, dark waters, do you look for Jesus, or do you blame Him?

_____

_____

_____

_____

_____

Have you ever felt like you were too far away for Jesus to reach you or your child?

_____

_____

_____

_____

_____

As you read through Matthew 14:22–33, what stuck out to you? What has God put on your heart?

_____

_____

_____

_____

_____

Treasures of the Week (Notes)

Your week ahead is going to be great. As you keep approaching God's throne, let's ask that He continues to fill your days with treasures. Everything about God is intentional, and all that we have read and heard thus far was to prepare our hearts for these last four weeks. He created you to walk on the water, and the first part to that is seeing Him in our boat. Let's see Him this week in the peaceful waters and in the raging. Our eyes are open, Lord. Show us what to write down this week.

_____

_____

_____

_____

_____

_____

_____

_____

_____

Week 14

Walking on Water

Immediately Jesus made the disciples get into the boat and go on ahead of him to the other side, while he dismissed the crowd. After he had dismissed them, he went up on a mountainside by himself to pray. Later that night, he was there alone, and the boat was already a considerable distance from land, buffeted by the waves because the wind was against it.

Shortly before dawn Jesus went out to them, walking on the lake. When the disciples saw him walking on the lake, they were terrified. "It's a ghost," they said, and cried out in fear. But Jesus immediately said to them: "Take courage! It is I. Don't be afraid."

<u>"Lord, if it's you," Peter replied, "tell me to come to you on the water."</u>

<u>"Come," he said.</u>

Then Peter got down out of the boat, walked on the water and came toward Jesus. But when he

saw the wind, he was afraid and, beginning to sink, cried out, "Lord, save me!"

Immediately Jesus reached out his hand and caught him. "You of little faith," he said, "why did you doubt?"

And when they climbed into the boat, the wind died down. Then those who were in the boat worshiped him, saying, "Truly you are the Son of God."

—MATTHEW 14:22–33 (NIV)

So let's get back to where we left off. Jesus shows up right before dawn, walking on the water. The disciples think He is a ghost. They cry out in fear, and Jesus tells them to not be afraid. When the disciples saw Him walking on the water, they were able to see that they didn't need to fear the raging waters. They had a Messiah that walked on top of the raging. And then after Jesus tells them not to be afraid, Peter begins to talk to Him. "Lord, if it's you," Peter replied, "tell me to come to you on the water" (Matthew 14:28 NIV).

I want to talk about Peter for a minute. Let's look at what he says first, "Lord, if it's you." He sees Jesus walking on the water, steps of miraculous wonder in the middle of a raging lake, and the first thing He does is question Him. Even Peter questioned if Jesus really is who He says He is, but what He said next tells me that Peter knew exactly who Jesus is.

He said, "If it's you, tell me to come to you on the water."

I think of my journey as a mom. I had a moment where I was in the boat of motherhood and the wind began to blow. The waves began to frighten me. But even in the storm, Jesus was calm. He walked up to my unsteady boat. I asked Him, "Jesus, are you really in this place? If you are here, then why don't you make it stop? Make the waves of uncertainty stop raging and tell the winds of this diagnosis to be calm."

He said to me, "Mattie, I don't need to tell the winds and the waves to stop. I need you to trust me even in the waves, even in the wind."

Peter didn't question Jesus's identity by telling Him to make the winds stop. He told Jesus that if it really were Him, then he wanted to walk on the water too. Peter knew that Jesus didn't create him to sink. He knew that if His teacher were walking on the raging waters, He could too. He knew that Jesus could calm the storm, but instead He asked for an invitation to join Him in the storm. He wanted to get out of a boat in rough waters and to follow Jesus, even in the wind.

Sometimes we expect Jesus to calm our storms, and perhaps at times He does, but I wonder if other times our storms aren't stilled right away because He wants us to walk through it and He wants our feet to experience walking above the chaos. I wanted to limit Jesus to just calming our storm, but He needed to me to see that I had another option.

Do you find yourself in a boat that endures the wind often? When your kids were diagnosed, did you talk to Jesus? Did you cry out to him, or were you silent? Maybe you didn't have the most loving words because while the wind was against you, you thought it was actually Him that was against you. Possibly He was the one you blamed when the wind hit your boat. Or perhaps He was your calm. We all endure the wind differently. We all see Him differently in our deep waters, but after reading Matthew 14:28–29, my hope is that no matter the wind's intensity, our pursuit to seek Him would be greater.

Jesus is who He says He is, and I believe He is waiting for you to say, "Jesus, if You are walking on these waters, if You are really on the water that is raging from the wind that is blowing against my boat, I want to come to You. Lord, call me to You because sometimes You calm the storms but other times You invite me to walk right through the wind, on top of the raging waters. Jesus, call me to You. Tell me to come. My trust in You is bigger than this wind. Lord, I want to walk through this wind. I want to feel these waves under my feet because with You I am above the fear of the waters beneath me!"

He may just look at you, sister, and say "come." He may just extend His arms, ready to catch you, and say, "Daughter, come."

He looked at me in the wind and said, "Mattie, come. Get out of the boat. You weren't meant to be sitting in this boat afraid. You were meant to walk on the water that is rocking it."

Prayer

Lord Jesus, We love You and thank You for always inviting us. You invite us into life with You, a life without fear, an existence where we can walk on the water that rages against us. Lord, You are a carpenter, and I ask that You would build the boats we sit in to be durable and strong. And I pray that just as Peter asked to join You on the waves, we would want to do the same. You are trustworthy, and we want to be with You always. Thank You for calming our storms and for inviting us into them. In Jesus's name. Amen.

Reflection Questions

Do you find it hard to talk to Jesus in the middle of your storms?

_____

_____

_____

_____

_____

When the wind starts blowing, do you put your trust in Jesus on the water or the boat? Where is your security when the wind blows?

_____

_____

_____

_____

_____

Peter asked Jesus for an invitation onto the water. He wanted to be with Jesus even if it meant stepping out of the boat. How could you step out of your boat today?

_____

_____

_____

_____

_____

When you find yourself in situations like Peter, would you rather God calm your storm or invite you to walk in it?

_____

_____

_____

_____

_____

How can you approach your journey this week with a trust in God that is bigger than your fear of the winds that blow your way?

_____

_____

_____

_____

Treasures of the Week (Notes)

As you approach God's throne this week, tell Him you want an invitation onto the waters that rage against your boat. He is faithful and trustworthy. I am praying that this week He shows you His faithfulness in the wind. He is good, and you are His. There is purpose in your story. Write down all that He is doing this week.

_____

_____

_____

_____

_____

_____

_____

_____

_____

_____

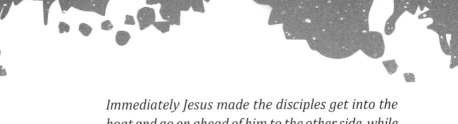

Week 15

Fearless Focus

Immediately Jesus made the disciples get into the boat and go on ahead of him to the other side, while he dismissed the crowd. After he had dismissed them, he went up on a mountainside by himself to pray. Later that night, he was there alone, and the boat was already a considerable distance from land, buffeted by the waves because the wind was against it.

Shortly before dawn Jesus went out to them, walking on the lake. When the disciples saw him walking on the lake, they were terrified. "It's a ghost," they said, and cried out in fear. But Jesus immediately said to them: "Take courage! It is I. Don't be afraid."

"Lord, if it's you," Peter replied, "tell me to come to you on the water."

"Come," he said.

Then Peter got down out of the boat, walked on the water and came toward Jesus. But when he

saw the wind, he was afraid and, beginning to sink, cried out, "Lord, save me!"

Immediately Jesus reached out his hand and caught him. "You of little faith," he said, "why did you doubt?"

And when they climbed into the boat, the wind died down. Then those who were in the boat worshiped him, saying, "Truly you are the Son of God."

—MATTHEW 14:22–33 (NIV)

To the woman who says, "Yes, Jesus, I trust You," this is for you. To the woman who wants to say, "Yes, Jesus, I trust You," but isn't sure yet if Jesus is trustworthy, this is for you. To the woman who doesn't yet know that Jesus made her to walk through the winds that are against her, this is for you. To the woman who cries out to Jesus when the wind hits her in the face and drowns her, this was written for you.

Peter said yes to Jesus, but it wasn't until after Jesus extended the invitation to "come." After this beautiful moment where Jesus said "come," Peter stepped out of the boat. As I am writing this today, Jesus spoke something so wise into my heart. "Peter asked to join me on the water and waited for my invitation before he stepped onto the water. He didn't just get out on his own. He wanted my direction. Peter wanted me to lead him in this situation. He asked, and he received, even in the middle of the lake. Because sometimes I come to calm the storm, but sometimes I come to invite you into the storm."

As Peter got out of the boat, he began walking toward Jesus, and he was walking on water. His feet were in miracle step with his teacher, and he was walking toward the Messiah on top of the waves fueled by the wind that was against him. What a moment this was for him! Can you imagine being the disciple who was walking on the lake toward Jesus?

Peter had a fierce trust in Jesus, but even Peter took his eyes off Jesus when the wind blew his way. The wind didn't stop beating against the boat when Peter got out of the boat. See, even in Peter's obedience to get out of the boat and walk toward Jesus, the wind didn't stop. Nope, it kept blowing. Fear continued to pursue Peter even as Peter was pursuing Jesus. When Peter's eyes were set on Jesus, he was walking on water. When his eyes shifted toward the wind, fear started to pull him under the water.

In our journeys, we are constantly invited to walk on the water, but so often after we get out of the boat, our eyes shift from Jesus to the wind that is blowing to sink us. We get out of the boat and say, "Yes, Jesus, we trust you," but then the wind blows, and we become afraid. The fear of the wind becomes greater than our focus on Jesus.

Anticipatory grief is a terrible wind, and it seems to drown me every time. Our daughters' diagnoses pose a very high risk for liver and kidney disease. We get them checked regularly to make sure that their livers and kidneys are healthy, but every time a child with their diagnosis passes away, the winds start to blow. Every time I see a mom who loses her child to Joubert syndrome, the wind tells me that I will be next, and I start to grieve a loss that hasn't even happened yet. My eyes shift from Jesus to the fear of losing my daughters, and I start to drown.

I forget that I have a six-year-old and a four-year-old who currently have healthy livers and kidneys. I forget all the promises Jesus has declared over our family, and I become consumed with the fear of never seeing my children again. I lose sight of what is true. Peter was walking on the water, and he lost sight of what was true. The wind hit him, and even though he was steady on the waves, the fear of what could happen to him in the wind actually began to drown him. Fear compromised what was going so beautifully.

God needed me to see these next words up close and make them personal: "He was afraid and, beginning to sink, cried out, 'Lord, save me!'" (Matthew 14:30 NIV). Ladies, we can't miss this.

When Peter was afraid and beginning to sink, he cried out. How many times do we sink before we look up and cry out? How many times do we let ourselves hit rock bottom before we ask our mighty God to move? How many times do we let the water fill our lungs before we cry out for Jesus to save us from the wind? Why do we scramble to try to save ourselves all the way to the bottom?

See, as Peter cried out, Jesus did what He always does. He immediately reached out His hand, and He caught Peter. Jesus doesn't want you to sink. He wants you to cry out before you ever go under. He wants your trust in Him to be so much stronger than the wind, so strong that you know you don't have to sink for Him to catch you.

You don't have to hit the bottom for Him to hear you. He's got you on the water, and He is ready to catch you before you ever go under. "Immediately Jesus reached out his hand and caught him. 'You of little faith,' he said, 'why did you doubt?'" (Matthew 14:31 NIV).

I am confident that Jesus didn't create us to sink, to doubt Him, or to settle for living at rock bottom. No, sisters, He created us to have a fierce trust and persevering faith. His promises are true, and His truth can shatter the doubt.

I don't know the diagnosis that your family has to navigate through, but I do know you were never meant to navigate through it alone. Jesus promises your children a hope and a future, and no diagnosis can get in the way of that. The winds of your child's diagnosis will try to sink you in fear, but Jesus wants your eyes on Him and your trust in Him so He can walk with you through the winds that are trying to take you under. And should you even begin to take your eyes off Him for a second, He will grab your hand and remind you of what is good and true before you even go under.

Let's be women who walk on the water and aren't afraid to cry out and need Him before we drown. Let's be women who have a fierce trust in our Savior and live our lives in the persevering faith that our Jesus will immediately be there to catch us when the winds blow. Never again will we let the fear drown us in the waters that we were meant to walk on.

Prayer

Hey, Jesus, thank You for immediately reaching out Your hand every time we cry out to You. I pray that we would always recognize Your hand that wants to keep us above the waves. I ask that every woman reading this would have a dependence on You that is so intense that the minute she starts to sink, she calls out to You. God, thank You for wanting to see us walk on the waters. I ask that You would call us to walk on the waters with You and with fierce trust and persevering faith we would get out of the boat. In Jesus's name. Amen.

Reflection Questions

What wind that comes your way has the greatest intensity? (Mine is anticipatory grief.)

_____

_____

_____

_____

_____

When Peter got out of the boat and trusted Jesus, do you think he felt the wind against him more or less than when he was in the boat? In moments where you trust God, do you feel the wind against you more or less?

_____

_____

_____

_____

_____

Do you usually cry out to Jesus as a first or last resort?

_____

_____

_____

_____

_____

Have you experienced Jesus immediately respond to you when you have cried out? When?

_____

_____

_____

_____

When is a time that Jesus caught you from drowning and the wind died down? Did you thank Him for his hand in the wind?

_____

_____

_____

_____

Treasures of the Week (Notes)

The wind comes to frighten us, but Jesus comes in the wind and invites us to walk through it. When we look down, we see the waves and feel the wind, but when we look up, our whole posture changes. We see Him, and when our focus is on Him, we can walk through anything. This week as the wind blows, look up at Him, and walk all the way to His throne. You are worthy of approaching His throne. In fact, this whole book has been His invitation for you to meet Him.

Ask Him this week for the courage to believe that you were made to walk on the water, that you were created to walk through the wind, and that He longs for you to run to His throne as often as you can. Let your heart experience Him this week, and as always, take notes along the way.

_____

_____

_____

_____

_____

_____

_____

_____

_____

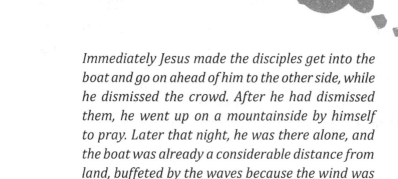

Week 16

Faithful Feet

Immediately Jesus made the disciples get into the boat and go on ahead of him to the other side, while he dismissed the crowd. After he had dismissed them, he went up on a mountainside by himself to pray. Later that night, he was there alone, and the boat was already a considerable distance from land, buffeted by the waves because the wind was against it.

Shortly before dawn Jesus went out to them, walking on the lake. When the disciples saw him walking on the lake, they were terrified. "It's a ghost," they said, and cried out in fear. But Jesus immediately said to them: "Take courage! It is I. Don't be afraid."

"Lord, if it's you," Peter replied, "tell me to come to you on the water."

"Come," he said.

Then Peter got down out of the boat, walked on the water and came toward Jesus. But when he

saw the wind, he was afraid and, beginning to sink, cried out, "Lord, save me!"

Immediately Jesus reached out his hand and caught him. "You of little faith," he said, "why did you doubt?"

And when they climbed into the boat, the wind died down. Then those who were in the boat worshiped him, saying, "Truly you are the Son of God."

—MATTHEW 14:22–33 (NIV)

I love bringing my daughter Hannah into my writing space. As she gets older, I delight in telling her about the work that God has given me in delivering His truth to mamas with unique journeys. I asked her if there was something that she wanted me to tell the mamas I am writing to, and she said, "Momma, ask them if they want to walk on the water." So if you have been wondering what inspired this four-week journey looking at the story of Peter and Jesus walking on the water, it was my daughter Hannah.

When she was four years old, she started asking me to tell her this story over and over again. She wanted every detail about the story. It was like she wanted to taste the water and be in the scene of this moment with Jesus. We always ended the story with the same question that she anticipated every time.

I would look right into her eyes and ask,

"Hannah, if Jesus asked you to walk to Him on the water, would you?"

She would close her eyes, and I could tell she was imagining every moment. She would open her eyes, and with a loud, excited voice, she would say, "Yes!" Sometimes I think she wanted me to tell her this story just so she could answer the question that always came at the end. She wanted the invitation to walk to Him. She wanted the thrill of saying yes.

Peter was in a boat full of men devoted to the mission of following Jesus. They were all different men heading in the same direction. They all stepped into the same boat and were all in the vessel as the wind was against it. They all saw Jesus approach them on the water before dawn and felt the waves under the boat.

As Peter was invited onto the water, the disciples watched. They sat in the boat that Peter stepped out of and watched Peter walk on the waves toward Jesus. Their eyes witnessed their brother in Christ conquer the wind as he took steps toward Jesus. They also saw Peter begin to drown from the fear that surrounded him, and they watched as Jesus was quick to rescue him after he cried out. "And when they climbed into the boat, the wind died down. Then those who were in the boat worshiped him, saying, 'Truly you are the Son of God'" (Matthew 14:32–33 NIV).

When Peter and Jesus climbed into the boat, the winds stopped, and praises broke out. Peter's willingness to join Jesus on the water showed these men once again that Jesus is exactly who He says He is.

As I was planning to write this last week of journeying with Jesus on the water, God wanted me to share something with you. "Your willingness to do this journey with me may be the only way others can see me." God has been so faithful in our journey. He's been there to invite me to walk on the water, and He's been there when I started to drown. I look at all He has done with our two girls, and I know that our journey wasn't just for ourselves. It was for others to witness His faithfulness and goodness.

Our journey is for others to see Jesus in the middle of our storm, and even in those days where I start to drown, others see His hand pull me up. People have watched our journey from the boat, and in the middle of the dark, windy waves, they have seen the Son of God show up and do the impossible.

You are a special needs mama, and your journey is unique to you. Peter's journey on the water was unique to him too, and it was full of purpose. Your journey on the water has purpose too. God wants to use your whole journey. With Him, nothing is wasted. Let's be mamas who see Him in our storms and mamas who get out of the boat when He says "come." Let's be mamas who raise our kids to trust the one that doesn't just call us to wait out the storms with our heads down in a rocking boat but actually calls us to walk on the water in the wind. Let's be mamas who teach our kids to be excited when the wind starts to blow because we know who will lead us through it. Let's be mamas who get empowered in our journeys because through our walks, others will get to witness His faithfulness and goodness.

My daughters inspire me every day. I have watched them struggle and thrive. I have experienced fears that have paralyzed me, and I've stayed in dark rooms with God for years. I've questioned where God has been in our journey, and I have been a daughter of His with little faith. Somewhere through the years I have realized that Jesus loves my kids more than I could ever comprehend. Their diagnoses will never take away who God says they are. Their diagnoses will never take away their places at God's table or change the purpose He planned for them long ago.

I am a woman who resides in Holland, and as people pass through from Italy, I hope they see one thing, a woman who walks on the water that rages against her. If people can see me walking on the water through the storm, they will see Jesus leading me through it— the Son of God who never fails to be in the middle of our storms; the Messiah who invites us to be above, not below; the Prince of Peace who is immediately present in our times of need; Jesus, our teacher, who is trustworthy and faithful. I hope that in our storms, others can praise Jesus, exclaiming that He really is who He says He is. Your journey may just be for those in the boat who are watching you trust Jesus as you step out of the boat and walk to the only one who can keep you above the waves!

Are you a mom who will join Jesus on the waters the next time the winds blow? Are you going to be a mom who raises kids to join Him too? Let's be women who praise God when we see our sisters in Holland, trusting Jesus on the waves, and let's be women who inspire their first steps. It's easy to trust Jesus in the calm, but our journeys often put us in the deep and the raging. Let's be women who walk on the waters there. Let's join Jesus wherever our boats take us, no matter the intensity of wind. I am ready to walk on the water. Are you?

Prayer

Heavenly Father, You are kind and present. You make it clear to us that we are meant to be above, not below, the waves that rage against us. Your hand keeps us above the waters, and Your Spirit leads us through them. I ask that You would keep Your women in Holland close. Never let them drown, but show them how it feels to walk on the water. Remind them, Lord, that Your promises to their kids will always be greater than the fears that try to drown them.

You are greater than every challenge they face, Lord. Thank You for this journey we were able to take together and for all the treasures You have placed in our hands. Lord, walking on the water is something we treasure, and we are grateful. I ask that You would show every woman in Holland how much You treasure them and their kids, and Jesus, I ask that You would place others around them to cherish them as the treasures they are. Continue speaking to us, Lord, and show us how You want to use our stories. We love You, Lord, and we thank You for being for us. In Jesus's name. Amen.

Reflection Questions

How do your kids inspire you?

_____

_____

_____

_____

_____

Who has God placed in the boat to watch as you step onto the water?

_____

_____

_____

_____

_____

When has been a time that others have seen Jesus in your journey?

_____

_____

_____

_____

_____

Who is someone that you can inspire to walk on the waves? How will you encourage that person?

_____

_____

_____

_____

_____

How does God want to use your story? Because, sister, I promise that He does!

_____

_____

_____

_____

_____

Treasures of the Week (Notes)

As we complete this Bible study, what has God been communicating? Throughout the week, ask God to show your heart what your next step is in sharing your story with others.

_____

_____

_____

_____

_____

_____

_____

_____

Conclusion

When I arrived in Holland, I was expecting Italy. I brought the wrong manual, and I didn't have a map. The language was different, and for many years, I had a lot of learning to do and few friends to learn with. I was isolated and angry. I thought my purpose was to have an enchanted life in Italy, and when my plane arrived in a place I never expected to be, I was lost, alone, and bitter. I didn't know how to be a special needs mom, and I surely didn't have a guide to teach me. I was left in a land I never expected to be with no help in sight. I spent years in the dark, looking down. I was weary, and I felt defeat daily. I was given two children who weren't promised milestones or a long life. My heart felt the excruciating pain of watching my children suffer and face hardships that I couldn't take away.

God needed me to look up. He needed me to see that He actually entered Holland before I ever arrived, and He vaulted the skies with a dazzling display of lights, all different and set apart to shine in the way they were created to, and although each star was different than the one it shined next to, together they shined with purpose, all stationed in their appointed places to shine light into darkness. God placed the stars in the black sky to ensure that I never had to encounter the dark. I may not have been able to buy a manual for raising a child with Joubert syndrome at Barnes & Noble, but I was able to buy a Bible, which has become a manual, a map, and a life-giving essential my soul requires daily. When I finally looked up, I was able to see Jesus standing in front of me with His hand stretched out, ready to be my guide. He partnered with Zachary and me as He began to show us how to navigate the mountains, waters, and dark nights of Holland.

After I looked up, I saw that Holland is a place where burdens are turned to blessings. When God asked me to start writing for the women in Holland, He continuously reminded my heart of this mantra, "Mattie, we are going after the few." Our God who created the many also cares so deeply for the few. He sees all of us in Holland, even when we feel the rest of the world doesn't. God pursues our hearts recklessly with a love that patiently waits for us to receive it. We are worth His stop.

God loves our children, and He created them with intention. We can cling to His promises and trust in His plans. All our kids were knit together in the womb with identity, belonging, and purpose. Whatever diagnoses our children have, it will never take away God's plans for their lives. We are in this together even when our stories shine differently.

In the days ahead as you raise your special stars, I pray that you would continue running to God's throne every morning and that you would ring in to Him often. I pray that your hands would be filled with treasure and that you would experience the lavished love He pours into us. On the darkest of nights, I pray that you look up at the stars and find great joy as you find the one that's set apart from the rest and remember the star that set apart that night to lead the shepherds to the manger where Jesus lay. Continue to walk in joy through the unknowns as you were anointed, appointed, and equipped for all the challenges you face. We are women who don't see just a glass of water. We see the wine. We have hope like that, and with Jesus, we see in high definition.

When people pass through Holland, my prayer is that they see us walking to Jesus on the waves that rage against our boats, and that they would see our faith in situations they would deem as impossible. Can I also mention one last truth about the people from Italy passing through Holland? They're in the dark too. They will never know the ins and outs of the hardships that mamas with special needs kiddos face. They could never understand some of the thoughts that keep us up at night and the defeat we encounter from time to time.

In those times, we have an opportunity to be a light to them, to show them that our God never leaves us. When they see a diagnosis, show them your hope! When they see fear for your child's future, show them your trust in God to give you days ahead to dance in! When they see your differences, remind them that God will use both of your stories differently! When they see the unknowns you face, share with them all the times God has been faithful thus far! And when they want to tell you about the hardships they face in Italy, listen and love them well. Encourage them with truth from scripture and insights you have learned along your way. Toss the division of your different hardships aside and remember that both Holland and Italy have different seasons and weather from time to time; however, both places experience black skies and vaulted starry hosts. Be a star that shines bright even when it seems set apart from the rest. Let your bursting light lead others to Jesus in Holland and in those times visiting with your friends in Italy! Shine on, sister!

CPSIA information can be obtained
at www.ICGtesting.com
Printed in the USA
LVHW091939101220
673848LV00021B/178

9 781664 206113